T0366758

# Indiana University
# Maurer School of Law

WELL HOUSE
BOOKS

# Indiana University Maurer School of Law

## The First 175 Years

**LINDA K. FARISS** *and* **KEITH BUCKLEY**

INDIANA UNIVERSITY PRESS

*This book is a publication of*

INDIANA UNIVERSITY PRESS
Office of Scholarly Publishing
Herman B Wells Library 350
1320 East 10th Street
Bloomington, Indiana 47405 USA

iupress.indiana.edu

© 2019 by Linda K. Fariss and Keith Buckley

*All rights reserved*

No part of this book may be reproduced or
utilized in any form or by any means, electronic or
mechanical, including photocopying and recording,
or by any information storage and retrieval system,
without permission in writing from the publisher.

This book is printed on acid-free paper.

*Manufactured in Canada*

Cataloging information is available
from the Library of Congress.

ISBN 978-0-253-04616-1 (hardback)
ISBN 978-0-253-04619-2 (ebook)

1  2  3  4  5   24  23  22  21  20  19

*This book is dedicated to the memory*
*of our friend and colleague*

**Colleen Kristl Pauwels**
*1946–2013*

# Contents

*We aim at nothing less, than the building up of a Law school that shall be inferior to none west of the mountains. We aim at the establishment of a Law school, that shall not only increase the Legal knowledge but elevate the moral & intellectual character of the Profession throughout Indiana.*

—Trustees of Indiana University, in a letter to Tilghman A. Howard *July 24, 1841*

# *Foreword*

INDIANA UNIVERSITY (IU) ENTERS ITS THIRD CENTURY IN 2020. It owes its existence to the vision and support of the state of Indiana, whose founding constitution declared in 1816 that "knowledge and learning generally diffused through a community" are "essential to the preservation of a free Government." In 1820, in Bloomington, our state laid the cornerstone for the university that would bear its name, and now, on the cusp of its bicentennial, Indiana University is our state's largest and most comprehensive university, and its Bloomington campus is a flourishing, humane, vibrant, creative, cosmopolitan, and connected center for passionate learning, powerful research, and local and global engagement.

A state with the vision to express constitutionally the nexus between education and democracy—and the foresight to found the future of its government at that nexus—would require a great law school. So would a university founded on principles of liberal education and research excellence. The Indiana University Maurer School of Law has more than lived up to these foundational ambitions, producing thousands of graduates who have formed not only the backbone of the state's commitment to rule of law but also a far-flung, global network of influence for the rule of law. Law graduates practice and lead in every one of Indiana's ninety-two counties, in most of our United States, and in countries on every inhabited continent.

School of Law graduates have shaped US Supreme Court jurisprudence as justices, law clerks, and practitioners. They sit on the federal bench and serve as justices of the supreme courts of Indiana and other states. They have served as elected representatives at every level of government, including in the US Senate and House of Representatives. They have been governors of Indiana, leaders of bar associations, and university presidents. Internationally, our graduates are justices on their nations' highest courts, government officials, and academic leaders. I have had the great fortune to meet with our alumni all over the state, country, and the world and to see their impact and, through them, the law school's impact on their communities and the global stage.

The fates of school and university have been intertwined throughout this history. The university's outstanding commitment to the arts, music, and the humanities made it possible to recruit excellent faculty from around the world to the heart of the country with confidence that they would be joining a vibrant community. Its development as a research powerhouse, with strengths in the sciences, social sciences, humanities, and other professions, attracted faculty members interested in both strong professional education and the cross-disciplinary links that shaped the school as an early and prolific participant in research situating law in society. Its long and perhaps surprising history of international engagement, dating back to summer study-abroad "tramps" through Europe that began in 1880, made possible the flourishing global programs and attractiveness to international students that have characterized the school for much of its history.

The law school's own international program began in the early twentieth century, when it graduated numerous students from the Philippines in 1907 and established its master of laws (LLM) degree in 1918. International engagement continues through the master's, doctoral, and juris doctorate education it provides to foreign lawyers today; the programs it nurtures around the world with other educational institutions; and the pathbreaking Stewart Fellows program that sends doctor of law (JD) students to summer legal placements around the globe. The university's strength in international education and its broad alumni reach, with over forty-five alumni chapters on every inhabited continent, allow potential international students to discover the law school and to find networks of fellow Indiana University graduates when they return home.

Indiana University's comprehensiveness and general excellence—it joined the prestigious Association of American Universities in 1909, just nine years after its formation—built the reputation that made the law school a credible founding member of the Association of American Law Schools (AALS). The strength of the university's schools and College of Arts and Sciences allowed the creation of programs and collaboration across the spectrum of research excellence and curricular innovation. Its position as one of the nation's great public research universities supported the law school's broad vision of what a legal education could be and permitted its students to thrive not only through the strength of their JD education but also through degree programs that joined a juris doctorate education with degrees in business, education, librarianship, public affairs, public health, environmental science, cybersecurity, communications, and the storied Russian and Eastern European program. Law students linked their JDs to doctor of philosophy (PhD) degrees, informing disciplinary depth with the rigor and values of a legal education. PhD students in turn minored in law, allowing them to place their disciplines in the context of broader societal concerns and practical policy implementation.

The Maurer School of Law has been generous in sharing its vision and expertise to many university initiatives, serving critical roles most recently in the development of new programs in intelligent systems engineering; art, architecture, and design; media; and global and international studies. The school is a vibrant contributor to the campus's intellectual life, convening and nurturing faculty from disciplines interested in legal institutions for decades through its Center for Law, Society, and Culture; bringing pathbreaking thinking about globalization and global legal institutions to the campus through the sharply imagined and cutting-edge work of the *Journal of Global Legal Studies*; supporting a growing campus climate of innovation through the Center for Intellectual Property Law and the Elmore Entrepreneurship Clinic; and developing the emerging discipline of constitutional design through the Center for Constitutional Democracy, which promotes the rule of law and seeks to make productive and participatory democracy an entrenched reality around the world. The law school led the campus to develop one of the earliest research centers devoted to the threats and challenges of cybersecurity, and it is a leader in addressing that issue educationally as part of an innovative multidisciplinary master's program with the Kelley School of Business and the School of Informatics, Computing, and Engineering. At one of the best research institutions in the country, the law school has played a leadership role both in academics and research, one that transcends its comparatively small size in the university's portfolio of programs.

Central to both Indiana University and the law school are commitments to diversity and inclusion. Both enrolled women and people of color at a time when many institutions closed their doors to these groups. Sarah Parke Morrison was Indiana University's first woman to graduate in 1869, just two years after IU became one of the first state universities to admit women. In 1892, Tamar Althouse became the law school's first female graduate. The first African American man to graduate from IU was Marcellus Neal in 1895, and the first African American woman to graduate was Frances Marshall in 1919. The law school graduated its first African American man, Sam Dargan, in 1909. Later, Juanita Kidd Stout came to Indiana from Oklahoma, where as an African American woman she could not pursue a legal education. She earned a juris doctorate from the law school in 1948 and went on to become the first African American woman elected judge in the United States as well as the first African American woman to serve on a state supreme court. These extraordinary graduates continue to inspire future students and faculty through institutions and programs like the IU Neal-Marshall Black Culture Center and the Juanita Kidd Stout Professorship.

As we approach the university's two hundredth year, a glance at Indiana University's leadership highlights the centrality of the Maurer School of Law to the mission and forward momentum of the university. Five of the university's fifteen vice presidents are faculty or graduates of the law school. In these roles, they shape academic excellence and policy on the Bloomington campus and regional campuses; strengthen the university's research initiatives; expand IU's global impact and reach; and protect and advance IU and its mission through legal advice and counsel. Our graduates also serve as members of the board of trustees and the IU Foundation Board, bringing their unique training to bear on envisioning the university's future and securing philanthropic support for its mission.

In the following pages, you will read chapters in the Maurer School of Law's rich history. It is a history that parallels that of the university that has nurtured it and has shaped that university in ways large and small. Both institutions have, in turn, shaped the world and our state, through the daily influence of their graduates and the power of their research. They both demonstrate the wisdom of the foundational commitment of that 1816 constitution, though those founders could scarcely have imagined the powerful ways in which that commitment would be expressed on a world stage and through hundreds of thousands of graduates two centuries on.*

*Lauren Robel*
EXECUTIVE VICE PRESIDENT AND PROVOST
VAL NOLAN PROFESSOR OF LAW
INDIANA UNIVERSITY

* Many thanks to Catherine Dyar for her ideas and assistance with this foreword.

# *Acknowledgments*

IN 2017, THE MAURER SCHOOL OF LAW CELEBRATED its 175th anniversary. Given this milestone, along with the university's approaching bicentennial in 2020, now seemed like the appropriate time to write its history. The school's 175-year history has been nothing short of remarkable, especially considering that its founding came at a time when there were no requirements for practicing law in Indiana other than being of "good moral character" and, preferably, male. There would be no formal requirements in Indiana until the 1930s. In light of this, we would like to first acknowledge state legislators who, in 1838, when changing the name of Indiana College to Indiana University, recognized that the mission of a great university must include professional education in law and medicine. We also must acknowledge the IU trustees who, three years before this, had the vision to approve the creation of a professorship of law, even if it took until 1842 to find someone willing to accept the position. To be sure, it was a rocky road for many years, but the leaders of the university and law deans, faculty, students, and alumni never gave up on the dream of a law school that was "inferior to none."

Between us, the authors have been present at the law school for the last quarter of its existence. Combined, we have six degrees from Indiana University, including one each from the Maurer School of Law, and we have spent our professional careers at this great law school, watching it grow globally and doing our part to ensure that the law library is prepared to meet the needs of the twenty-first century. For this reason alone, we are proud to be the people to record the school's history. But we also wished to honor our colleague and friend Colleen Kristl Pauwels, the director of the law library from 1978 until her retirement in 2011, who was, among her many roles, the unofficial historian. She cared deeply about the school and its past and planned to write a history in her retirement. Sadly, she passed away in 2013 before she could accomplish this, so we have written this partly for her. We hope she would be proud.

We have many people to thank for their role in making this book possible. First of all, we thank Austen Parrish, dean of the Maurer School of Law, for his constant support and enthusiasm for the school's history. The many photographs in this book would not have been possible without the assistance of four people: A big thanks goes to Katy Bull, archive and digital preservation specialist at the Jerome Hall Law Library, who was unfailingly helpful with the many requests we made from the library's photo archive. Bradley Cook, photograph curator for the University Archives at the Wells Library, provided numerous photos from the vast collection, as well as much-needed advice and encouragement. James Boyd, director of communications at the Maurer School of Law, was always helpful in finding and identifying photos from his archive, especially those that document more recent activities. Last but not least, we thank Karen McAbee, business manager for the Jerome Hall Law Library, who used her years of experience to help locate elusive photographs that we knew existed but just could not find.

Doing the research for this book would have been much more cumbersome without the Jerome Hall Law Library's digital repository. A special thanks goes to Nonie Watt, the repository's project manager and assistant director for technical services; Dick Vaughan, acquisitions librarian, who oversees many of the collections within the repository and is the self-proclaimed "idea man" for the history collection; and, once again, Katy Bull, who is responsible for organizing and maintaining the print archives as well as aspects of the digital repository. We would like to also thank Rebecca Bertoloni-Meli, head of circulation and patron services for the Jerome Hall Law Library, who was so helpful in retrieving materials that were not readily available. Kristin Leaman, bicentennial archivist for the University Archives, retrieved valuable files about the law school.

Ken Turchi, assistant dean for communications and administration at Maurer, gave much-needed advice and support, and Andrea Havill, assistant dean for external affairs and alumni relations at Maurer, was always quick to assist with questions about our alumni. We would like to thank Kelly Kish, deputy chief of staff in the Indiana University President's Office and bicentennial director, for her assistance with historical and background materials on IU officers. Finally, we would like to thank Peggy Solic, acquisitions editor at IU Press, for her guidance, advice, and encouragement.

Linda would like to thank her husband, Jim Fariss, and daughter, Katie, for their support and encouragement throughout this project. She would particularly like to thank Jim for his advice and willingness to read and reread the manuscript when he must have been weary of doing so. Keith wishes to thank his wife, Patty Lawson-Buckley, for her cheerful support during the writing. He would also like to express his sincere gratitude to the entire staff of the Jerome Hall Law Library for their encouragement and patience.

# *Introduction*

IN 1842, WHEN INDIANA UNIVERSITY HAD BEEN IN existence for only twenty-two years, there were no educational requirements for the practice of law in the state of Indiana, and there would be none for nearly another one hundred years. In spite of this, the state legislature and the board of trustees believed in the importance of professional education as part of the mission of the university. And so, on December 5, 1842, David McDonald gave the inaugural lecture for the Indiana University School of Law, challenging the new law students to enter the profession if they desired to "promote the best interests of society" (McDonald 1843, 22). In spite of considerable success in those early years, the financial struggles were mighty, and the law school was suspended in 1877.

Fortunately, the story does not end there. Students and others clamored for the reestablishment of the school, and in 1889, the president and board of trustees decided the time was right to revive it. The struggles were not over, but this time the school was able to weather them and flourish. In the early years, the growing school moved to various buildings, quickly outgrowing its space, until it settled in Maxwell Hall in 1908, remaining there until 1956, when it finally moved into its first specifically constructed building, now called Baier Hall.

By the turn of the twentieth century, the law school was growing and diversifying its student body. The first woman had graduated from the school in 1892, and the first African American graduate was in 1909. The law school's first international students, a group from the Philippines, arrived in 1904. From this time on, international students were a constant presence. As a nationally recognized law school, Indiana University School of Law became a charter member of the Association of American Law Schools in 1900, and when the American Bar Association (ABA) first accredited law schools in 1923, the school received Class A standing, the highest offered by the organization.

For a time during the mid-twentieth century, Indiana University's school was considered one of the top law schools in the nation, under the leadership of Bernard Gavit, the longest-serving dean in the school's history. Legendary faculty like Hugh Willis, Fowler Harper, Jerome Hall, Ralph Fuchs, John Paul Frank, and Austin Clifford added to its reputation. Of special note is Hall's pioneering role in the law and society movement, which continues to be an essential part of the law school's identity today. But by the 1970s, once again plagued by financial troubles and serious talk of closing the flagship school, the law school fought for its very existence. Under the leadership of Dean Sheldon Jay Plager, and with the support of the university and a devoted alumni base, the school weathered yet another storm and gained momentum, receiving much-needed funding, adding to and updating its physical space, increasing admission standards, and hiring faculty among the best in the nation.

With strong and dedicated leadership, the School of Law not only persevered but emerged into the twenty-first century stronger than ever. During the 1990s, under Fred Aman's deanship, the school turned its attention to becoming a global law school, developing relationships worldwide. Lauren Robel, who became the first female dean in 2003, inspired strong support from alumni and the university, securing transformative gifts from alumnus Mickey Maurer and the Lilly Foundation. With this funding, the school was able to recruit the best students and foster scholarly productivity from the Maurer faculty, propelling it to a position among the best public law schools in the country.

From humble beginnings in 1842, the Maurer School of Law today is not only a top-tier national law school but also a global school that has developed partnerships with leading institutions in the world and an alumni base that spans the globe. Thanks to top-notch faculty, the school has developed nationally recognized programs in areas such as intellectual property law, tax law, and international law. But at the heart of the school is the desire to promote the best interests of society, to prepare students not only to practice law but to also take a leadership role in providing solutions to society's most pressing problems. This was true on December 5, 1842, and it remains true today.

# Indiana University
# Maurer School of Law

FIG. 1.1. Seminary Square campus as it looked at time of founding of the law department. *Left to right:* Seminary Building (circa 1825), First College Building (1836), and Laboratory (1840). *Artist: William B. Burford. Circa 1850. IU Archives P0022535.*

# 1 | THE BEGINNING
## *1842–77*

"WE ARE ENTERING UPON AN EXPERIMENT not before attempted in this seat of learning—an experiment, which touches a variety of interests dear to the University, and dear to the legal profession of the State of Indiana" (McDonald 1843, 5). So began the inaugural address by Judge David McDonald, the first professor of law, on December 5, 1842, marking the birth of the Indiana University School of Law, the first public law school in the Midwest and the ninth-oldest law school in the nation. This event was the official beginning, but the idea for a law school at Indiana University had been conceived many years before.

Indiana University was founded in 1820 as the Indiana Seminary (*Laws of Indiana*, 1819, 82–83). In the earliest days, only Latin and Ancient Greek were taught. In 1828, the legislature changed the school's name to Indiana College in order to better reflect its goals to teach youth "American, learned and foreign languages, the useful arts, sciences, and literature" (*Laws of Indiana*, 1827, 115–19). In 1838, the Indiana legislature once again changed its name, this time to Indiana

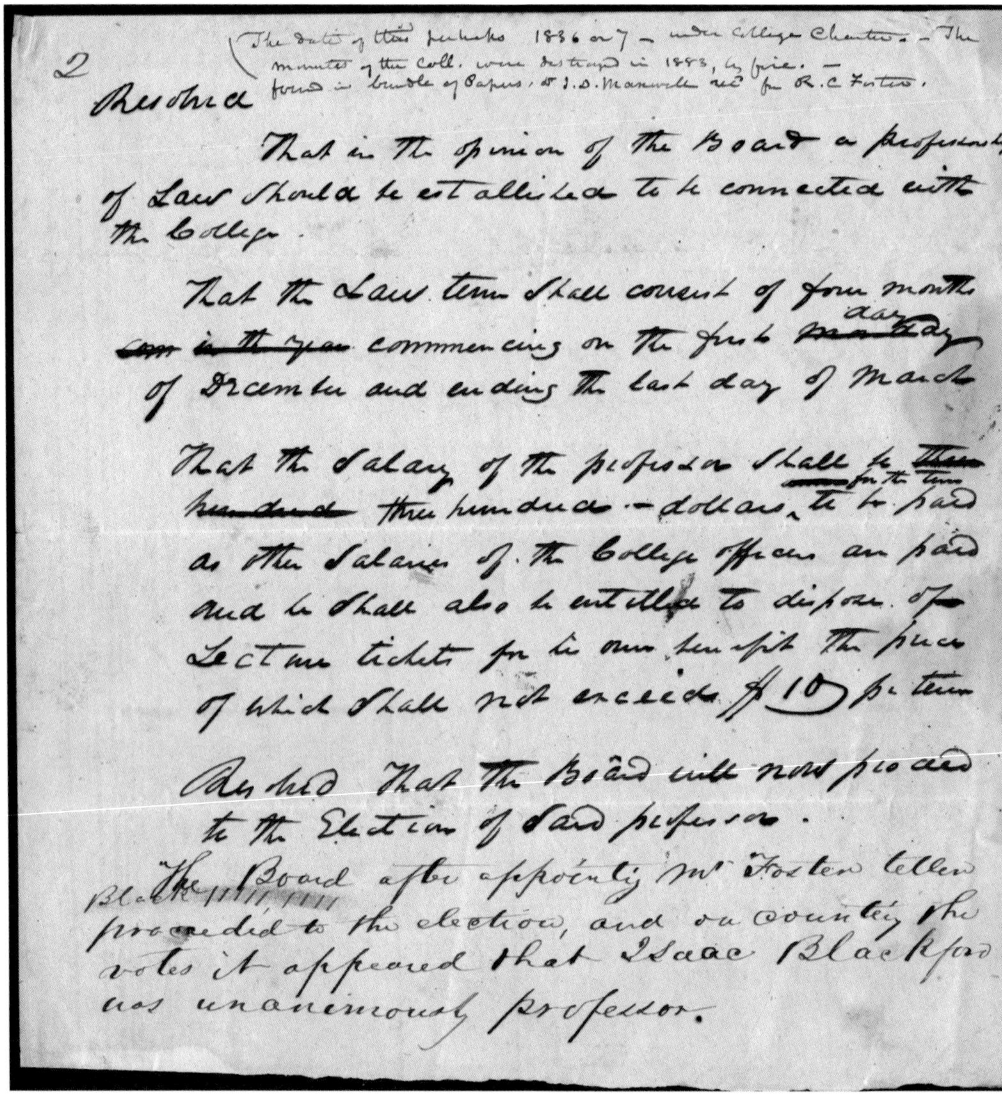

2 (The date of this perhaps 1836 or 7 — under College Charter. — The minutes of the Coll. were destroyed in 1883, by fire. — found in bundle of papers, of J. D. Maxwell rec'd fr R. C. Foster.

Resolved

That in the opinion of the Board a professorship of Law should be established to be connected with the College.

That the Law term shall consist of four months ~~com in the year~~ commencing on the first ~~Monday~~ day of December and ending the last day of March

That the Salary of the professor shall be ~~three hundred~~ three hundred dollars for the term to be paid as other Salaries of the College officers are paid and he shall also be entitled to dispose of Lecture tickets for his own benefit the price of which shall not exceed $10 per term

Resolved That the Board will now proceed to the Election of said professor.

The Board after appointing Mr Foster teller proceeded to the election, and on counting the votes it appeared that Isaac Blackford was unanimously professor.

Black ////////

**FIG. 1.2.** Piece of paper that escaped the fire of 1883, the only evidence that trustees approved the establishment of a law professorship in 1835. Document is dated September 31, 1835 (assume it was actually September 30, 1835). *IU Archives.*

University, stating that the school's mission was for the education of youth in the "American, learned and foreign languages, the useful arts, sciences (including law and medicine) and literature" (*Laws of Indiana*, 1837, 294–98). This was the first mention of the study of law as part of the mission of the university.

Although most official university records were destroyed in the fire of 1883, a piece of paper containing a resolution by the trustees from the year 1835 establishing a professorship of law survived, apparently having never been placed with the official records. A notation on the resolution indicated that Judge Isaac Blackford, a member of the board of trustees, was elected to the position, but he declined for unknown reasons. Three years later, after the legislature added the study of law to the university's mission, the position was offered to Judge Miles G. Eggleston, who also declined for unspecified reasons. No other formal offers were extended until 1841, when the trustees offered the position to General Tilghman A. Howard.

According to the minutes of the board of trustees for July 1841, the trustees sent a letter to Howard in which they expressed the desire for "the building up of a Law school that shall be inferior to none west of the mountains. We aim at the establishment of a Law school that shall not only increase the Legal knowledge but elevate the moral & intellectual character of the Profession throughout Indiana."

FIG. 1.3. First College Building, site of the inaugural lecture given by David McDonald on December 5, 1842, in the chapel. Law classes were held in this building until it was destroyed by fire in 1854. *IU Archives P0022519.*

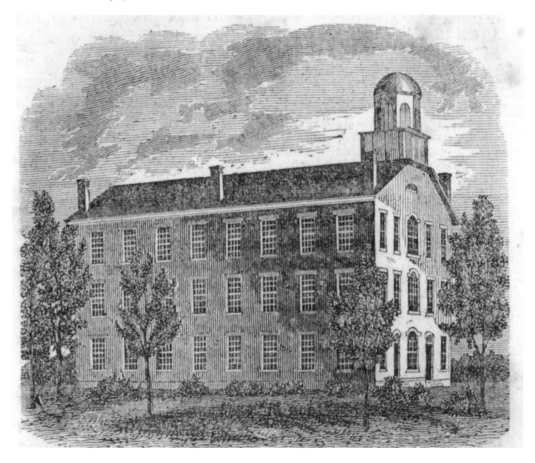

The letter went on to say, "In a word we wish the Law Students of Indiana University to be so trained, that they shall never, in the attorney forget the scholar and the gentleman." Howard was offered the fees paid by the law students as well as $400 the first year and $300 annually after that. The trustees anticipated the enrollment of fifteen to twenty students the first year. As an added incentive, the trustees declared that the law professor would be independent, answerable directly to the board.

Although Howard was flattered by the offer, he declined, indicating that it would require him to make too many sacrifices. Finally, in June 1842, the board of trustees secured the appointment of Judge David McDonald as the first professor of law, at a salary of $1,000 per year, and all fees paid by law students would go to the university. The trustees were pleased to finally see the law department come to fruition, believing that it would add greatly to the standing of the university.

After years of attempts, the law department was officially launched with the lecture given by McDonald on December 5, 1842. As was the custom, the lecture was open to the public and held in the university's chapel. There is no record indicating how many new law students attended this lecture, but two years later, five students graduated in the department's first class. McDonald ended his address with a challenge to the new students of law: "And now, young gentlemen, if you are willing to endure the labor of mastering this noble science; if you are willing to spurn the trifles which engage the time and affections of too many of our youth; if you glow with honorable emulation; if you desire to be distinguished among your fellow citizens, and useful to our beloved country,—here is a field worthy of our labor—a field, in which you may, at once, gratify a laudable ambition, and promote the best interests of society" (McDonald 1843, 22).

Law department applicants were not required to have a high school diploma, the university requirement for admission, but instead needed to produce satisfactory testimonials of good moral character. The trustees originally envisioned that students would complete two years of study with two terms in each year, although it was possible to enter as a senior if the student had made sufficient progress in the study of law elsewhere. The terms were intended to consist of four months each, but the trustees reluctantly agreed, at least temporarily, to reduce the requirement to a single three-month term each year, beginning on the first Monday of December. McDonald suggested this change in order to encourage student enrollment and to accommodate his schedule riding the circuit, which began the first Monday of March and ended on the last day of November. It was understood that if the legislature allowed a change in his court schedule, the term would be increased to four months, beginning on the first Monday of November. With this change, the trustees reduced his salary to $100 per month during time that classes were in session.

Instruction consisted of lectures on various branches of the common law and equity jurisprudence, examinations, and moot courts, which were held every Saturday. There students were given exercises in pleading and arguing legal questions, and the judge also gave an opinion on the questions of law involved in the exercise. Textbooks used were listed in the *Catalogue* for 1845 as *Blackstone's Commentaries*, *Story's Commentaries on the Constitution*, *Chitty on Contracts*, *Stephen on Pleading*, *Kent's Commentaries*, *Chitty on Bills*, *Chitty on Pleading*, *Greenleaf's Evidence*, and *Mitford's Equity Pleading*.

Though there is no existing record of how many students attended the first lecture, in 1843 there were fifteen law students: six seniors and nine juniors. The first graduating class in 1844 consisted of five men: Francis Patrick Bradley, who practiced in Washington, Indiana; Joseph Blair Carnahan, who practiced in southern Indiana; John M. Clark, who practiced in Vincennes, Indiana; Jonathan K. Kenny, who practiced in Terre Haute, Indiana; and Clarendon Davisson, who practiced in Petersburg, Indiana, in addition to being a newspaper editor in Bloomington, Indianapolis, Chicago, and Louisville and appointed consul in Bourdeaux, France (Wylie 1890, 310). By 1847, the

## JUDGE DAVID McDONALD

David McDonald was born in Millersburg, Kentucky, in 1803 and moved to Indiana when he was fourteen years old. He was a school teacher in Washington, Indiana, when he met a lawyer who encouraged him to study law. McDonald read the law, was licensed to practice in 1830, entered private practice in Washington, and was also a member of the Indiana General Assembly from 1833 to 1834. In 1838, he was elected judge of the Tenth Judicial Circuit of Indiana and served in that capacity for fourteen years.

McDonald became the first professor of law at Indiana University in 1842, serving in that role until 1853, when he resigned to return to private practice in Indianapolis. Upon his resignation, the university presented him with an honorary LLD degree. In 1856, he published *McDonald's Treatise*, a book designed for justices of the peace and constables, which was reprinted many times. On December 12, 1864, President Abraham Lincoln nominated him to a seat on the US District Court for Indiana. McDonald was confirmed by the US Senate on December 13, 1864, and received his commission the same day, serving until his death on August 25, 1869, in Indianapolis. He is buried in Crown Hill Cemetery in Indianapolis.

FIG SIDEBAR 1.1. Judge David McDonald, first law professor, 1842–53. *IU Archives P0079349.*

# LIFE IN BLOOMINGTON IN THE 1800s

The following is an excerpt from a letter published in the *Alumnus*, written by William Pitt Murray (LLB; 1849), describing travel to Bloomington, the town, and the law department in 1848 (Murray, "The University Fifty Years Ago," *Alumnus*, February 1899, 6–10).

*Dear Sir:*

*Bloomington, fifty years ago, was a country village of the Hoosier type, without side-walks or graded streets,—mud, mud everywhere. Its home and business houses were of the most primitive kind—the old State University building, built without regard either to ancient or modern architecture or convenience. The village was off the high-ways and lines of travel—even more inaccessible than New York or San Francisco, if you desired to travel pleasantly.*

*I remember but as yesterday the bleak, chilly Thursday afternoon in November on which I left my home in Centerville, Ind., for Bloomington, taking my seat in a stage coach. This was then the only means of public travel. There was but one railroad in the State of Indiana, that from Madison to Indianapolis. It is sixty-two miles from Centerville to Indianapolis, yet it was not until nearly noon on Saturday that we were driven up to a small hotel in Indianapolis . . . and were then told that we would have to remain in Indianapolis until Monday morning, as no stage went out to Bloomington until then. About four o-clock Monday morning a rapping at the door awoke me, when I was told that the stage (that is, if a three-seated open wagon, drawn by two Hoosier ponies could be called a stage) for Bloomington was at the door. . . . It not only rained but poured that day,—mud and slush everywhere. We were compelled to walk every now and then to assist the ponies. At a log building, a way-side inn, we had breakfast, and near midnight we drove up to Orchards' Hotel, in the college town. . . . The next day [Robert H.] Milroy and myself, who had arranged to room together, commenced looking around for winter quarters. . . . we secured board with the Misses Henderson not far from the college building, where we had a good clean room; good feather beds; . . . wood furnished in sled lengths, which we had to cut into fire-wood lengths, and carry up to our room,—and all of this for one dollar and twenty-five cents a week. . . .*

*Society in Bloomington fifty years ago was, no doubt, different from now. Some of the young men wore jeans suits and cow-hide boots. The amusements were not as numerous as now, perhaps—mostly confined to church sociable, and now and then some tramp would come along and deliver a lecture of Phrenology or some kindred subject. The Judge, every two or three weeks, would, at the close of his Friday lecture say, "Young Gentlemen, I will be at home tomorrow evening." We knew what this meant—a dozen or more village girls would be there. We had fun as a matter-of-course and sometimes turned the house upside down, but it was all right: the Judge never appeared to see what was going on. Some two or three of the young men got caught, and the population of Bloomington was reduced to that extent. . . .*

*Very respectfully yours,*

WILLIAM PITT MURRAY

department was successful enough to add a second professor, Judge William T. Otto. According to the 1847 *Catalogue*, its success "exceeded the expectations of its friends" (15).

The law department was successful, but the university had constant financial difficulties. At their October 1846 meeting, the trustees considered closing the department due to insufficient funds. Instead they sent a communication to McDonald asking if he would consider continuing to teach with only the fees paid by law students, as well as a room and firewood, as his sole compensation. Although unhappy with this proposition, McDonald agreed to continue for the time being without his salary.

Financial problems were not the only obstacle to the law department's success. Indiana approved a new state constitution in 1851, which included Article VII, Section 21, stating "every person of good moral character, being a voter, shall be entitled to admission to practice law in all Courts of justice." This was likely included to placate Jacksonians, who were concerned that educational requirements would lead to lawyers becoming the ruling class. The lack of formal education requirements left many potential lawyers without incentive to obtain law school training. Numerous attempts were made to change this provision to no avail, until the 1930s, when the state finally set down specific educational requirements for the practice of law as well as requirements for the passage of a state bar exam.

In the late 1840s, a problem arose between President Wylie and Judge McDonald over the discipline of a law student. The student was charged with violating certain rules and regulations of the university, although what specifically happened is unrecorded. The president called the student to appear before the faculty on the matter. Hearing this, McDonald sent a letter to the president stating that the university had no authority to discipline a law student and that only he or Otto was so authorized. While jurisdiction was still being discussed, McDonald investigated the complaint against the student and issued a reprimand. While no formal agreement was ever reached, it was generally agreed as a matter of courtesy that the law department would handle the discipline of its students. Following this, for unknown reasons, the law department was omitted from the university catalog for 1851 and 1852, prepared under the supervision of the president, who died in late 1851. Whether or not this controversy was the cause of the omission, the law department was never left out again (Miller 1950, 15–17).

McDonald and Otto were held in high esteem by their students. McDonald was described as a very kind man with a great interest in the welfare of his students. Otto was unmarried and treated students like companions and associates. William Pitt Murray, 1849 graduate of the law department, wrote, "And now after fifty years, I revere and honor the memory of these men with love and affection. It

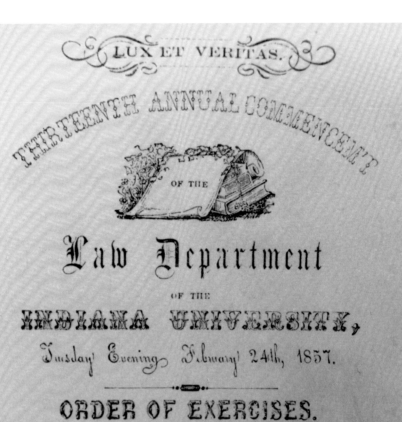

LUX ET VERITAS.

THIRTEENTH ANNUAL COMMENCEMENT

OF THE

# Law Department

OF THE

## INDIANA UNIVERSITY,

*Tuesday Evening February 24th, 1857.*

## ORDER OF EXERCISES.

### PRAYER.

The Federal Constitution.
D. D. BANTA,.....................................B'oomington, Ind.
The Law of Happiness.
HENRY P. BRAZEE, Jr.....................Cannelton, Ind.
Duties of Citizens.
JAMES W. BROWN,..........................Marion. Ind.
Rights of Citizens.
OMER F. ROBERTS,..........................Wye Hill, Ind.
Ancient Laws.
EDMUND JAEGER,...................Lawrenceburgh, Ind.

Address to the Class and Degrees Conferred,
BY DR. DAILY,.............President Indiana University.

**Music by the Bloomington Saxe Horn Band.**

**FIG. 1.4.** Commencement program for the class of 1857. David D. Banta, who would become the law school's first dean in 1889, was one of the graduates. *Jerome Hall Law Library Archives.*

## LAW GRADUATES IN THE CIVIL WAR

According to university records, twenty-two graduates of the law department fought in the Civil War, although the number could be higher. An additional fifty law graduates, who received their degrees after the Civil War, also served.

Francis Neff (LLB; 1853) was the only law graduate reported killed during the war. He enlisted in the Union army in 1861 and was a lieutenant colonel at the time of his death. Neff participated in the battles of Fort Donelson, Pittsburgh Landing, Stone River, Chickamauga, and Kennesaw Mountain, where he lost his life on June 24, 1864 (Barbour 1920, 488).

The Cox brothers were an excellent example of how the war pitted family members against one another. Jesse Towell Cox and Joseph Cox, twin brothers, were born on March 21, 1821, in Orange County, Indiana. Jesse Cox (LLB; 1868) served as a hospital steward and surgeon in the Union army and was taken prisoner for a period of time at the surrender of the forces at Munfordville, Kentucky, in 1862. His brother, Joseph Cox (LLB; 1854), served as a major in the Confederate army. Captured on a scouting expedition in Tennessee in 1863, he was held prisoner of war at Nashville and Johnson's Island, in Lake Erie, until the close of the war.

Following the war, Joseph returned to Paoli and practiced law before returning to Dallas, Texas, in 1880, where he had worked prior to the war. Jesse practiced law in Kokomo and Bloomington, Indiana, and Groesbeck and Dallas, Texas. Jesse Cox died on August 26, 1882, in Paoli, Indiana, and Joseph Cox died on August 10, 1899, in Rockwall County, Texas. By all accounts, their opposition in the war did not interfere with their brotherly affection (Wylie 1890, 340).

was their ambition to make lawyers out of their students, who would rank among the first in the country" ("The University Fifty Years Ago," *Alumnus*, February 1899, 7).

Otto remained at the law department until 1852, when he resigned to return to private practice. He headed the Indiana delegation to the Republican National Convention in 1860 and was considered instrumental in delivering Indiana to Abraham Lincoln, who later appointed him to a position with the US Department of Interior. In 1875, Otto was named the eighth Reporter of Decisions for the Supreme Court of the United States, which he held until 1883. It was during his tenure that, for the first time, case volumes were not named after the reporter. Because of this, he is sometimes referred to as the "first anonymous reporter." Otto died in Philadelphia in 1905.

In 1853, one year after Otto's resignation, McDonald also resigned to return to private practice. Following McDonald's departure, Judge James Hughes was appointed professor of law and held the position until 1857. He took a one-year leave

**FIG. 1.5.** Composite of the law class of 1871. In addition to students, the photo includes President Cyrus Nutt, Professor Samuel Perkins, and Professor Baskin Rhoads. *Jerome Hall Law Library Archives 010\2014.COMP.43.*

of absence in 1856 after being elected to the US Congress, and Ambrose Carlton, bachelor of laws (LLB; 1849), temporarily took his place. Following the completion of his leave of absence, Hughes resigned from the university and was succeeded by Colonel James R. M. Bryant, who remained until 1861, resigning for an appointment in the Union army after shots were fired at Fort Sumter. Judge George A. Bicknell succeeded Bryant.

Law department enrollment had fluctuated in the years prior to the Civil War. According to an article in the student newspaper at the beginning of the war in 1861, only five students were in the department (*Indiana Student*, February 15, 1868, 6). During the first year of Bicknell's leadership, the enrollment increased to ten in spite of the war, and it numbered fifteen the following year. After the war, Bicknell continued to lead the law department, where he was considered an excellent teacher and had a stellar reputation. During his tenure, the department grew in number, with twenty members in the class of 1870 and thirty-one in the class of 1871.

Following Bicknell's resignation in 1870, several people served short terms as professor of law: Judge Samuel E. Perkins, Judge Delana R. Eckels, Judge D. W. LaFollette, and Cyrus F. McNutt (great-uncle to Paul V. McNutt, who later would become dean of the law school and governor of Indiana). Bascom E. Rhodes was also chosen to be professor of law in 1870, where he remained until the department closed.

No official records indicate where law classes were held during this period, although they moved around and at times were held off campus. When the department was first established in 1842, law classes were likely held in the building known as the First College Building. After the fire of 1854 destroyed this building, classes met in a small room on the second floor of the old Seminary Building (Woodburn 1940, 247). Space constraints necessitated that classes be held wherever space could be found, which sometimes included the halls of the Athenian and

FIG. 1.6. Monroe County Courthouse, built in 1826 and expanded in 1850s. This is how it would have looked in the early 1870s, when law classes were held on west side of downtown square. 1856. *IU Archives P0074382.*

FIG. 1.7. Science Hall, constructed 1874. Law classes returned to campus upon its completion and were held here until the law department was suspended in 1877. Circa 1876. *IU Archives P0022533.*

Philomathean literary societies. There are also accounts of classes in law offices in the town. In a 1921 article, the *Indiana Daily Student* reported that Judge Robert W. Miers of Bloomington (LLB; 1871) spoke at a Demurrer Club meeting where he recollected that classes were held in "a tiny room over a store on the west side of the square" ("Judge Miers Addresses Demurrers Last Night," *Indiana Daily Student*, January 14, 1921, 1). By 1874, law classes were back on campus following the construction of Science Hall, where they remained until the department closed in 1877.

In terms of enrollment, the law department was quite successful. In the 1870s, graduating classes in law were sometimes larger than other departments (at this time, law graduates were not counted with the regular student body). In spite of this, in 1877, the trustees voted to "suspend" the law department. The reasons were both philosophical and financial. In 1875, Lemuel Moss became president of the university; not a proponent of professional education, he preferred instead to focus on collegiate education. In a statement published in the university catalog in 1877, Moss wrote that he believed professional schools of law and medicine should be graduate schools, requiring a college education as preparation for a graduate program (*Catalogue* 1877, 44). He was not incorrect; however, no schools of law or medicine in the country required a college degree, and it would be many years before it was the norm.

The university also needed to hire additional faculty but lacked financial resources, as the legislature had already reduced salaries for existing faculty, producing, it was felt, conditions making it difficult to secure competent instructors for the law department. At the time of its closing, there were 41 students in attendance and 384 alumni, including many prominent public figures and jurists. Among the graduates were Samuel H. Buskirk (LLB; 1845), Indiana Supreme Court justice; Willis A. Gorman (LLB; 1845), appointed governor of the Minnesota Territory; and Arthur C. Mellette (LLB; 1866), elected first governor of South Dakota. Even with this temporary setback, the experiment had been a success.

**FIG. 1.8.** Law students in class, Science Hall. Circa 1876. *IU Archives P0071810.*

FIG. 2.1. Old Crescent in 1898. From left to right: Maxwell Hall, Owen Hall, Wylie Hall, and Kirkwood Hall. During the period of this chapter, the law school was located in each of these buildings. *IU Archives P0035211.*

# 2 | A REBIRTH

### 1889–1933

EVEN THOUGH THE TRUSTEES MADE THE decision to suspend the law department in 1877, the desire for a law school never faded. The general public and students in particular began calling for the reinstatement of the law school. In 1885, David Starr Jordan, the new president of the university, turned his attention to the student demands.

During the time that the law department was closed, a significant event happened to the university. In July 1883, Science Hall was struck by lightning, resulting in a devastating fire. Along with its important contents, the entire library, including the law library, was destroyed. The trustees were faced with a difficult decision. The campus was inadequate for future growth, and the fire renewed the call by some to move the university to another location within the state. At their meeting on August 23, 1883, the trustees acted quickly to declare that the university would

remain in Bloomington, but it would be moved to another location. A twenty-acre tract of land called Dunn's Woods was purchased for the new site. Using insurance proceeds and a $50,000 donation from Monroe County, construction was begun on the new campus, and the first classes were held there in 1885.

Against this backdrop, Jordan asked the board of trustees to consider the possibility of reestablishing the law school. A committee was formed to study the request, and in June 1886, they reported that the consideration of a law school would have to be postponed due to lack of funds. The university was engaged in a disagreement with the state, in which the state was refusing to pay a semiannual installment, and the committee felt that the financial status was too uncertain to commit to a law school at that time. It took two more years before the idea came before the trustees again. In 1888, another committee was appointed. This time the trustees approved the idea of reinstating the law school, but funds were still lacking.

Finally, in 1889, the trustees agreed on reestablishing the law school and hiring two professors, one of whom would be the dean. Law classes were to begin the following September. Perhaps in response to the standoff between Judge McDonald and President Wylie over jurisdiction of law students, at the March 1889 meeting, the trustees also established that "law students shall be subject to the same general regulations as students in other departments." To say the students were enthusiastic would be an understatement. The *Indiana Student* proclaimed, "The School of Law has been exhumed from its unsought grave and placed on a firm foundation, so that once more ample facilities for a legal training are offered to all who may desire to avail themselves of the opportunity" (*Indiana Student*, October 1889, 4).

The next order of business was to hire faculty for the new department. The trustees chose Judge David Banta to be the first dean of the new school at an annual salary of $2,500. At the time, Banta was president of the board of trustees and, at Jordan's suggestion, resigned from the board to accept the deanship. In 1890, the trustees appointed the second professor, Ernest W. Huffcut. After his resignation in 1892, Huffcut was replaced by William P. Rogers, a prominent attorney.

Born in 1833 in Johnson County, Indiana, David D. Banta had both bachelor of science (BS; 1855) and LLB (1857) degrees from Indiana University. An advocate of higher education for women, Banta taught for one year at the Monroe County Female Seminary before moving to Franklin, Indiana, in 1857, where he set up a law practice. Elected circuit judge in 1870, he enjoyed an excellent reputation as both a lawyer and judge. Banta was a trustee at the university from 1877 until 1889, serving as president for many of those years.

FIG. 2.2. David D. Banta, first dean of the law school, 1889–96. Circa 1890. Photographer: A. G. Hicks. *Jerome Hall Law Library Archives 010\2014.HIST.24.*

As before, the study of law was an undergraduate program, consisting of two years study with two terms each year. The trustees added a third summer term in 1890, corresponding with the regular university schedule. Tuition was set at $12.50 per term. Initially, admission requirements for the law school were not the same as the rest of the university, where a high school diploma was required. For the law school, applicants had to be at least eighteen years old, pass an exam demonstrating their ability to write and speak good English, and show a reasonable proficiency in the common school branches. By 1890, high school graduates were excused from entrance exams. However, it was announced in 1896 that every applicant was required to take an entrance exam in English composition and that if applicants failed the exam, they were required to take an English course at the university. By 1899, admission standards for law were the same as the rest of the university.

Classes began in September 1889 with thirty-two students enrolled. As previously stated, the campus had moved from its original location to Dunn's Woods, the site of the present-day campus. The first buildings erected on the new campus were Wylie Hall and Owen Hall. Library Hall, later to be named Maxwell Hall, was completed in 1890. When first opened, the law school was housed in cramped space in Owen Hall (*Indiana Daily Student*, February 21, 1908, 2). After Library Hall was completed, the law school occupied the second floor of its east wing.

In 1890, law students organized their first club, which they named the Forum. Originally conceived as a literary society for law students, it was established to deal with subjects that would increase their knowledge of the law and give them training that would help with practice, such as preparing briefs, arguing fictitious causes, and discussing laws. It rapidly grew in popularity and membership and even had a motto: "Keep Pegging Away." By 1892, it had evolved into the Forum

# TAMAR ALTHOUSE—FIRST WOMAN GRADUATE

Born in New Harmony, Indiana, in 1872, seventeen-year-old Tamar Althouse arrived at Indiana University fresh out of high school to become the first woman graduate of the law school. From the accounts of the day, Tamar was well respected and active in university life. According to a student newspaper account, when she attended a meeting of the literary societies to represent the Philomathean Society, the law students came as a body to cheer on Althouse and the law student representative for the Forum. As stated in the article, the law students "paid honor to the Forum representative, and the only lady law specialist in the west, by frequent and hearty applause" (*Indiana Student*, February 1892, 97).

Upon graduation in 1892, Althouse moved to Evansville, Indiana, and was admitted to the bar in 1893 at the age of twenty-one. She joined the law office of J. E. Williamson, becoming the first woman to practice law in Vanderburg County. In addition to her law practice, she also served as court reporter for Vanderburg County from 1903 to 1915, served on the staff of the state speaker of the house Al Venaman, and was on special duty to the Indiana Public Service Commission in 1924.

Althouse had a passion for women's rights, which was first evidenced in an article she wrote for the *Indiana Student*. She stated, "But to whatever source woman's recognition in the past may be attributed, in the future higher education will form the 'open sesame' for our women to all honors, all distinctions, all happiness, all opportunities, that are in any way desirable in after life" (Althouse, "A Question," *Indiana Student*, November 1892, 11–12). In Evansville, she sought out female colleagues in other professions, and in 1914, she was one of the founding directors of the Women's Rotary Club

in Evansville, the first in the country. Women's rotaries all over the country were founded on the principles of the Evansville club.

Althouse retired from practice in the mid-1920s to devote time to the care of her husband, Frederick J. Scholz, who had become disabled. She remained involved in her professional work on a reduced basis for several more years and died in November 1936 at the age of sixty-four. In 1992, on the centennial of her law school graduation, she was inducted into the Academy of Law Alumni Fellows.

FIG. SIDEBAR 2.1. Tamar Althouse, 1892. Photographer: Summers, Bloomington, Indiana. *Photo credit: Indiana Historical Society P0477.*

FIG. 2.3. Group of law students with Dean Banta in 1891. Pictured is Tamar Althouse, first female graduate of the law school. *Jerome Hall Law Library Archives 010\2014.COMP.44.*

Court, and its main purpose was mock trials and practice in parliamentary law. It is uncertain how long this organization lasted, but its final mention in the newspaper was in October 1894.

In 1870, Ada Kepley, a graduate of Union College of Law (now Northwestern University School of Law), became the first woman to graduate from a law school in the United States. Twenty years later, and only one year after reopening, Indiana University School of Law admitted its first woman, Tamar Althouse. In 1892, Althouse became the first female graduate of the school. She was well accepted and respected by her male classmates. In reporting on the law school graduation exercises, the *Indiana Student* stated, "Miss Althouse realized that the practice of law would be a thorny road for her to travel, but being a peculiar combination of feminine gentleness and American pluck, she is determined to succeed. All who know her are anxious for her success" (W. S. Tipton, "Law Class of 1892,"

FIG. 2.4. William Perry Rogers, dean of the law school, 1896–1902. *Photo courtesy of IU Archives. Jerome Hall Law Library Archives 002\2013.FAC.143.*

*Indiana Student*, October 1892, 19–20). By the close of the century, four women had graduated from the law school, receiving LLBs. In addition to Althouse, they were Elizabeth Hunter Van Nuys (1894), Genevieve Winfield Kelly (1895), and Alice Harper Ballard (1899).

Quickly outgrowing its space, the law school moved into the newly constructed Kirkwood Hall in early 1895, sharing the building with numerous other departments. Located on the first floor, the law school had two lecture rooms and a large room for the library. All was not well with the new building, as there were complaints about inadequate heating and ventilation. The ventilation in the law library was a particular problem, as described in the *Indiana Student*: "From twenty to thirty spend the entire afternoon in this room, and the air becomes unwholesome. To open the windows interferes with the system of heating, but that seems to be the only recourse" (*Indiana Student*, December 3, 1895, 112). Some things never change!

On April 9, 1896, Banta passed away at his home in Bloomington. On the announcement of his death that Thursday, all departments at the university were closed until the following Monday. That year the student yearbook published a memorial written by Professor William P. Rogers honoring Banta, stating, "As a citizen he stood for, and sought to maintain, all that is highest and best in government; as a lawyer he enjoyed the fullest confidence of the public, and the highest respect of the court; as a judge he was painstaking in research and fearless in announcing his conclusions; as a teacher he was magnetic, clear and inspiring. His life was well rounded, and was an exemplification of a genuine Christian gentleman—the highest style of American manhood" (*Arbutus*, 1896, 127).

On Banta's death, William P. Rogers assumed the deanship, and Judge George L. Reinhard was appointed professor of law. Rogers was born in 1857 in Brown

County, Indiana. He attended Indiana University from 1877 to 1880 but was unable to finish at that time. He practiced law from the early 1880s until 1892, when he received his LLB from Indiana University and became a professor of law. He received his bachelor of arts (AB) degree from IU in 1895.

## A New Century

The law school was well situated to face the challenges of the twentieth century, with more demand for a formal education and more requirements imposed on legal education. The enrollment for the 1901–2 academic year was 144, and the

**FIG. 2.5.** Moot courtroom, Wylie Hall. 1904. Photographer: Bass & Woodworth. *IU Archives P0034550.*

FIG. 2.6. George L. Reinhard, dean of the law school, 1902–6. *Photo courtesy of IU Archives. Jerome Hall Law Library Archives 002\2013.FAC.142.*

course of study was increased from two to three years. Once again facing a shortage of space, the school moved to the third floor of Wylie Hall.

As the demand for legal education grew throughout the country, the need for national standards was becoming apparent. The Association of American Law Schools was formed in 1900. The Indiana University School of Law was one of thirty-two charter members of this organization. Standards for membership required a high school diploma for admission, a degree program at least two years long, and access to a library with *US Reports* and local state reports. In 1905, AALS increased the length of time for a degree from two years to three years, which the Indiana University School of Law had already met.

In 1902, William Lowe Bryan became the president of the university. One of his first tasks was to replace Dean William Rogers after he resigned to become dean at the Cincinnati Law School. Bryan appointed Judge Reinhard to succeed Rogers, and Enoch Hogate was chosen as professor of law. In addition to being named dean, Reinhard was also given the title of vice president.

George L. Reinhard was born in Bavaria and came to the United States when he was fourteen years old. He attended Miami University in Ohio for two years after serving in the Union army during the Civil War. Reinhard practiced law in Kentucky before moving to Rockport, Indiana, to continue his practice. He served as prosecutor and circuit judge prior to coming to the law school in 1896. In 1897, he received a doctor of laws (LLD) from Miami University and, in 1899, a master of arts (AM) from Indiana University.

During Reinhard's tenure, law schools across the country were changing their methodology of teaching. Professor Langdell of Harvard had introduced the "case method" in 1870. Instead of lectures and recitations from textbooks, students read cases and discussed the findings of the court. By this time, the Indiana faculty

**FIG. 2.7.** Reinhard Club members. 1902. *Jerome Hall Law Library Archives 010\2014.HIST.50.*

were using a combination of textbook method and case method in their teaching. In order to learn more about how schools were teaching using the case method, Reinhard visited several prominent law schools, including Harvard, Boston, Yale, Columbia, and Pennsylvania. Enthusiastic about what he observed, on his return, he wrote an article in which he described the effect the case method had on the classroom: "Neither the dogmatic statement of the text nor that of the instructor is any longer blindly followed, and the spirit of freedom of discussion and independence of thought pervades every well-conducted class in the law school" (Reinhard 1904, 166). After this, the law school phased out traditional styles of teaching in favor of the case method.

In 1902, law students formed another club, the Reinhard Club, named in honor of Dean George Reinhard. The club was established to encourage extemporaneous

## SAMUEL SAUL DARGAN— FIRST AFRICAN AMERICAN GRADUATE

Born in South Carolina in 1869, Sam Dargan attended Cornell University and MIT before graduating from Purdue University with a BS in science in 1905. Immediately after, he began his legal studies, becoming the school's first African American graduate in 1909. Following graduation, Dargan elected to remain in Bloomington and accepted a position at the law school. From 1908 until he retired in 1948, he held the title of curator of the law library, and he also operated a business selling law books to students. Beloved by students and faculty alike, he was given the title "Father of the School of Law" by Dean Paul McNutt.

Dargan owned several boarding houses on the west side of campus, where he leased rooms to African American students who were not permitted to occupy student housing until after World War II, and his houses became social centers for the students. One of his buildings, the Dargan House near campus, was the first residence for African American female students. He was active in the community, serving on the Bloomington draft board and also on a committee of prominent African Americans who developed ways to help Bloomington's black population secure jobs on national defense projects.

Dargan retired in 1948 at the age of seventy-six but continued coming to the school on a regular basis until shortly before his death in November 1954. The law school closed for two hours on the day of his funeral to allow students, faculty, and staff to attend. In 2009, on the centennial of his law school graduation, he was inducted into the Academy of Law Alumni Fellows.

FIG. SIDEBAR 2.2. Samuel S. Dargan. 1908. Photo taken for *Arbutus*. Photographer: Shaw, Bloomington, Indiana. *IU Archives* P0030485.

speaking ability. At each meeting, a topic would be presented, and sides were chosen to debate the issue without any previous preparation. Annual membership was limited to fifteen law students. The club lasted for several years after Reinhard's death, and its last mention was in the 1911 *Arbutus*.

Law school enrollment and diversity continued to increase in the early twentieth century. In a report on the law school that appeared in the December 19, 1905, edition of the *Daily Student*, it was stated that enrollment for the 1904–5 academic year was 187 students with a projection of 250 for the following year. There were sixty-three counties in Indiana with one or more students in the law school, as well as students from Ohio, Kentucky, Illinois, Minnesota, Iowa, Utah, and California ("School of Law Keeping Pace with Rapid Progress so Noticeable in All Departments of the University," *Daily Student*, December 19, 1905, 1). During this time period, Samuel Saul Dargan became the first African American to graduate from the school in 1909, and Masuji Miyakawa, graduating in 1905, was the first Asian American graduate. The school was also experiencing its first international representation with a group of students from the Philippines (see chap. 6).

In an effort to further boost enrollment, the law faculty adopted a combined degree program proposed by Reinhard in 1904, where a student could receive

FIG. 2.8. Maxwell Hall, home of the law school from 1908 until 1956. 1910. *IU Archives P0020049*.

FIG. 2.9. Enoch G. Hogate, dean of the law school, 1906–18. *Photo courtesy of IU Archives. Jerome Hall Law Library Archives 002\2013.FAC.116.*

both an AB and LLB in five years. Prior to this, law could not be taken as a major in the Department of Liberal Arts. Under Reinhard's plan, students could take law as a major and meet the requirements of both the Department of Liberal Arts and law school in five years instead of the seven years previously required.

Once again facing a shortage of space, the law school jumped at the opportunity to claim Maxwell Hall when it was announced in 1905 that funds had been appropriated for the construction of a new library building. In fact, Reinhard, the law faculty, and law students held a celebration in anticipation of moving to Maxwell Hall, even though no promises had yet been made for the space. In an address to the board of trustees, Bryan made the case for the law school's claim to Maxwell Hall, stating, "I trust you will not be disposed to disappoint them" (Myers 1952, 464). The trustees agreed, and an addition was constructed on the northwest side of Maxwell Hall in 1907 to give the law school more classroom space. When the new library building was completed in late 1907, the school immediately moved to Maxwell Hall, just in time for the beginning of classes in January 1908.

Sadly, Reinhard died unexpectedly in July 1906 before seeing the law school move. He was succeeded by Enoch Hogate, who had been a member of the law faculty since 1903. Born in New Jersey, Hogate came to Indiana with his family when he was fifteen years old. He attended Allegheny College in Pennsylvania, receiving his AB in 1872, AM in 1875, and an honorary LLD in 1909. Before joining the law faculty, Hogate was clerk of the Hendricks County Court and had been elected to the state senate in 1896.

During Hogate's tenure, law schools were increasing admission and graduation requirements, in part because academic organizations were pushing for stronger requirements for professional schools. Shortly after moving to Maxwell Hall, the

## SHOULD WE SIT, OR SHOULD WE STAND?

In January 1912, the senior laws decided that it would be a new custom for all law students to stand when their professor entered the classroom and to remain standing until he was seated. The general sentiment was in favor of this custom, as it was in vogue at other law schools and some courts in the country. Professor Hepburn was quoted as saying, "Other law schools have customs, while not exactly like this, are similar to it. The University of Virginia has a custom of applauding the professors when they enter the classroom. In court rooms it is the general custom for the members of the bar to stand when the Judge enters the room. The general idea of this is not to show respect to the professor or judges, but to the Law which they represent. I believe that this would be a fine thing to establish here and I am heartily in favor of it" ("New Law Tradition Makes a Big Hit," *Daily Student*, January 11, 1912, 1).

However, this was a short-lived custom! Many students either forgot to stand or did not agree with the decision. One student surmised that students were so worried about being called on that they forgot to stand. Some students felt that the school was too democratic for such a custom. In November 1912, the student newspaper reported that, after a few days, it grew old and was dropped.

law faculty voted to increase entrance requirements to require one year of college work in 1910 and two years in 1911. Before this could be announced, the Association of American Universities issued a ruling stating that members must require two years of college work for admission to professional schools. Not wishing to compromise their membership, the trustees moved up the date for the new requirements to one year of college in the fall of 1909 and two years in the fall of 1910. The law school feared that the suddenness of this decision would cause a dramatic drop in admissions. Fortunately, this did not happen, and Hogate announced that enrollment dropped by only twenty-one students in 1910, after the two-year requirement went into effect.

Although there is evidence that it existed in some form prior to the turn of the century, the Demurrer Club was organized as an official club of the law school in 1913. Formed to be similar to the Skeleton Club at the medical school, its stated purpose was to promote friendship and sociability among those interested in the study of law at Indiana University. Membership was open to all law and prelaw students as well as faculty of the law school. In the 1920s, the Demurrer Club, along with the legal fraternities, was very involved in trying to get a dormitory for law students. Members of the club and fraternities went as far as having an option on a house and named it Inns of Court. According to the student newspaper,

FIG. 2.10. Law faculty in 1915. *Left to right:* William S. Beeler, Jesse M. LaFollette, Dean Enoch Hogate, Charles Hepburn, and John Lewis Baker. *Jerome Hall Law Library Archives 010\2014. HIST.1915.*

FACING TOP, FIG. 2.11. Future US Supreme Court Justice Sherman Minton (*middle*) with fellow I-Men. 1915. The I-Men's Association was formed in 1913 for IU athletes who received a letter in their respective sports. Minton played baseball and football while at IU. *Jerome Hall Law Library Archives 010\2014.HIST.27.*

FACING BOTTOM, FIG. 2.12. Moot courtroom, Maxwell Hall. 1917. *IU Archives P0026479.*

law students were attempting to raise funds, but no further mention of its success could be found, and the Inns of Court never became a reality.

In March 1917, Hogate suffered a serious stroke as he was leaving a classroom and had to temporarily relinquish his responsibilities as dean. By June 1918, it became apparent that he would not be able to resume his duties, and Professor Charles Hepburn was appointed to succeed him. Born in Virginia in 1858, Charles McGuffey Hepburn was the grandson of William Holmes McGuffey, famous for the McGuffey's Reader, which became the standardized reading text for most

## LEGAL FRATERNITIES AT THE LAW SCHOOL

From an early date, there was interest in forming legal fraternities at the school. In 1897, a group of law students, with the help of Professor Reinhard, founded Delta Alpha Delta, the school's first legal fraternity. Unfortunately, it only lasted for one year. Law students attempted to revive the fraternity in 1899, hoping to interest other law schools in opening a chapter. They apparently were unsuccessful, as no other mention was made of this fraternity. The John W. Foster chapter of Phi Delta Phi was established at the law school in 1900 and is still an active fraternity at IU.

Founded at the University of Michigan in 1869, Phi Delta Phi was considered the best legal fraternity in the country. In 1911, the Gamma Eta Gamma fraternity chapter was established at the law school, having been founded at the University of Maine in 1901. In 1926, the fraternity even had a house on east Kirkwood where up to twenty-five members could live. In 1928, a third national fraternity, Delta Theta Phi, founded in 1900, was installed, and the IU chapter was named for David D. Banta. This is still a large and active fraternity.

schools in the US during the mid-to-late nineteenth century. Hepburn received an AB degree from Davidson College in North Carolina, LLB from the University of Virginia, and LLD from Miami University. He practiced law in the Cincinnati area before joining the faculty at Indiana University in 1903.

Many law schools were expanding degree options, and the law faculty at IU had been anxious to offer graduate work leading to a master of laws or doctor of law degree for several years. Harvard considered offering a JD in 1902, and the University of Chicago was the first law school to award a JD in 1903. The requirements for a JD degree at IU were finally announced in the *Law Bulletin* for 1917. As with the

FIG. 2.13. Charles McGuffey Hepburn, dean of the law school, 1918–25. *Photo courtesy of IU Archives. Jerome Hall Law Library Archives 002\2013.FAC.115.*

## CANES OR HATS (OR MAYBE A MUSTACHE)?

In the early 1900s, the senior law students would pick out distinctive dress for the class, such as pants or a shirt in a particular color. In 1916, for example, they chose to wear a light corduroy vest with purple trim. In 1914, there was even a rumor that they had chosen the mustache as a custom, when it was noticed that many members of the class were sporting hair on their upper lips!

For a period of time, beginning in the early 1920s, senior law students carried distinctive canes of a particular color bearing their name and class date. Although nobody is sure of the origins of this tradition, some believe that it started at Harvard and other law schools followed suit. The first mention of canes at IU was in an October 1921 article in the *Indiana Daily Student*, which reported that the senior laws were carrying them as "distinctive badges" of senior law status. Professor LaFollette was quoted as saying, "They lend a certain amount of distinction which some of you might not acquire otherwise" ("Senior Laws Scorn Umbrellas to Sport Canes on Rainy Day," *Indiana Daily Student*, October 8, 1921, 1). The paper also reported that it was understood that the canes would remain outside the classroom in order not to cause a commotion.

In 1926, there was demand for a distinctive article of dress for all law students, and the students chose a gray hat with a purple band, although some were not happy with the color combination. For a couple years, they even wore a hat similar to a ten-gallon cowboy hat. In 1930, the senior laws decided to abandon the cane in favor of a gray hat with a purple band. However, the vote was overruled, and eighteen seniors decided to carry canes, while the rest would wear the hats!

Over the years, seniors stopped wearing the hats and carrying the canes, but bowlers and canes remained a symbol for law students for years to come, especially in connection with the law-medic rivalry.

FIG. SIDEBAR 2.5. Law students distributing bowler hats and canes. 1956. Although the custom that classes would choose a distinctive hat and cane had disappeared, law students still brought them out for special occasions, such as the law-medic football game. *IU Archives P0079322.*

LLB, students had to complete three years of law school to graduate. However, to qualify for a JD, candidates must have already earned an AB degree, achieved high academic ranking in law school, and completed a thesis. The first students to graduate with a JD were Roscoe O'Byrne and William Winfred Seagle in 1918. At this time most students in the US still opted for the LLB, and it would be the 1960s before the JD became the standard degree for law students. The JD became the standard degree at Indiana in 1968.

As expected, enrollment declined dramatically during World War I, reduced to as few as twenty-six students for one term. Additionally, three members of the faculty left to join the war effort, decreasing the faculty numbers by half. Professors Morton Campbell, Paul McNutt, and Frank Seavey entered the military as commissioned officers. Fortunately, all three returned to the law school following the war.

## Post–World War I

Immediately following the war, enrollment rose to 130, and by 1921, enrollment had reached 200 students, the largest ever. The rapid increase was partly due to the relaxation of admission standards for returning soldiers. On request of the law faculty, the trustees agreed to admit on probation discharged soldiers who had six months of service in the army or navy if they had completed four years of high school but less than two years of college work. If they completed the first year with an average grade of C, they were eligible to become candidates for the LLB degree.

The law school made curricular changes and added a new joint degree in the early 1920s. The School of Law and the School of Commerce and Finance (now the School of Business) agreed to offer a joint degree for which students could receive both BS and LLB degrees in six years. It was thought that this would fulfill a desire for legally trained professionals in business fields. In 1923, Hepburn announced what was described as a "drastic revision" in the law curriculum. Under the changes, only first-year courses would be compulsory, and students could choose their courses for the second and third years. The courses required for the first year were Equity, Property, Moot Court, Code Pleading, and Indiana Practice (*Indiana Daily Student*, November 13, 1923, 1).

In 1922, a committee of senior law students was formed to consider organizing a law alumni association in cooperation with the university alumni association. Members of the committee were Gilbert P. Adams, Samuel Cleland, James Meyer, Walter Treanor, and Posey Kime. At the law commencement dinner held on June 2, 1922, Posey Kime reported on the committee's findings and urged his fellow

**FIG. 2.14.** Class of 1921 in front of Maxwell Hall. Dean Hepburn can be seen sitting cross-legged (*first row, second from left*) in the light-colored suit. *IU Archives P0079351.*

classmates to become members of the law alumni association, which was to be formed the following fall (*Indiana Daily Student*, June 3, 1922, 4).

The Indiana University School of Law, along with the other leading law schools in the United States, had been advocating for increased standards without the support of the American Bar Association. Finally, in 1921, the ABA voted to adopt standards for law schools and directed the Council on Legal Education to publish the names of law schools in compliance. The newly adopted standards related not only to admission requirements but also to other aspects of a school, such as its library and number of faculty. Over the years, these standards were expanded to cover nearly all areas of a law school. In 1923, the Indiana University School of Law received Class A standing from the ABA, one of only thirty-nine law schools in the country to receive this honor. Schools had to meet four requirements for Class A standing: two years of college for admission to the law school; three years

# LAW-MEDIC RIVALRY

For many years, students of the law and medical schools engaged in a friendly rivalry that included sports challenges, verbal insults, and pranks. Since the schools were originally located side by side, law in Maxwell Hall and medicine in Owen Hall, it made for a natural rivalry. Although football was the main focus, it was not the only sport in which they challenged each other. They were also known to extend their feud to the baseball diamond and basketball court.

By far the biggest rivalry involved the law-medic football game. First mention of this was in the student newspaper in 1912, when the freshmen medics challenged the freshmen laws to a football game. It must have been a success, because by 1915 it was described as the "annual" law-medic football game and was held during homecoming weekend. By the 1920s, it was in full swing, and both sides enjoyed taunting each other prior to the games, from posting insults in the student newspaper, to pointing wooden guns at the buildings, to promising a brass band to accompany the team (which never materialized). They even had a trophy called the Thundermug, which went to the victor.

Of course, both sides also had distinctive apparel that they wore while marching to the games and taunting each other from the sanctity of their buildings. The Mad Monks of Maxwell, as the laws were called, wore dark suits and bowler hats, and carried canes, and the medics wore lab coats and carried large bones. Sometimes the laws would also have ducks with them to taunt the "quack" medics.

The game remained a beloved tradition, and the rivalry continued until the medical school moved off the Bloomington campus to Indianapolis. The last big law-medic homecoming game was held in 1957, as the freshmen medics were moving to Indianapolis the following year. Games continued for a few years, but they were much less intense than in years past.

FACING TOP, FIG. SIDEBAR 2.6A. Laws and medics on parade with university band. View looking to north side of the downtown square, law students appear behind the band, and medical students are rounding the corner. 1913. *IU Archives P0033706.*

FACING BOTTOM, FIG. SIDEBAR 2.6B. Law football squad in law-medic football game. 1932. *Jerome Hall Law Library Archives 010\2014.HIST.10.*

**FIG. 2.15.** Carmichael's Collegians, a jazz group formed by Hoagy Carmichael while at IU. Hoagy is at the bottom on the piano. 1924. *IU Archives P0020770.*

of full-time study for a law degree; an adequate library, available to the students; and sufficient full-time teachers. Around the same time, in 1925, Indiana's standing among the finest law schools was further enhanced when it was granted a petition to establish a chapter of the national law honor society, the Order of the Coif. At the time of its installation, there were only about twenty chapters in existence.

The top 10 percent of the graduating class was eligible for election. This remains one of the highest honors for a law student today.

By this time, major law schools had begun publishing a law review. The *Harvard Law Review* was first published in 1887, and Yale began its law review in 1891. As early as 1911, it was reported that the law school desired to publish a "law magazine," but funding was not available and there was little hope that it could be obtained. In 1916, the school began to seriously consider the possibility of a law journal, and Professor Hepburn was asked to investigate what would be required. After consideration of the costs, it was decided that the journal was not feasible at the time. The law faculty did not give up hope and once again asked for authorization to launch a journal in 1918. Still nothing happened.

The establishment of a law journal was a top priority for Dean Hepburn, so he negotiated with the Indiana State Bar Association to jointly publish a journal. After much discussion, the proposal was finally brought to the board of trustees, who approved the joint endeavor in 1925. It was agreed that the bar association would take financial responsibility and the law faculty and students would take charge of the editorial work. Paul Sayre was the first faculty editor, and the student board of editors, chosen by the faculty based on class standing, included Pearl Lee Vernon, the only female law student at the time. The first issue of the *Indiana Law Journal* was published in 1926. It was not until 1948 that the journal was edited entirely by students.

Believing that the journal as proposed would put an undue burden on an already-too-small faculty, the law faculty had expressed disapproval of Hepburn's concept to Dean Hepburn and President Bryan. They also favored a publication that focused on scholarly articles and not state bar issues. Because of the faculty's unhappiness with how Hepburn handled the law journal negotiation and with Hepburn's advanced age, Bryan offered him the title of research professor if he would resign as dean, which Hepburn accepted (Pauwels 2000, xiv). At the time, only three other members of the IU faculty had this title: C. H. Eigenmann, dean of the Graduate School; A. L. Foley, chair of the Physics Department; and James A. Woodburn, professor emeritus of history and former chair of the History Department ("McNutt to Succeed Hepburn as Executive of Law School," *Indiana Alumnus*, May 9, 1925, 7). This new role suited Hepburn, as he was a nationally regarded scholar and a life member of the American Law Institute. On his death of a heart attack in July 1929, Bryan stated, "Indiana University and the American bar lose in him a man of high distinction, and those who knew him best lose in him a treasured friend" (*Indiana Daily Student*, July 22, 1929, 1).

Paul V. McNutt was chosen to succeed Hepburn, becoming the youngest dean in the school's history at thirty-five years old. He had come to Bryan's attention

**FIG. 2.16.** Paul V. McNutt, dean of the law school, 1925–33. *Photo courtesy of IU Archives. Jerome Hall Law Library Archives 002\2013.FAC.130.*

through his university committee activities and letters he had written about how to move the law school forward. A young and energetic successor to Hepburn was very appealing. McNutt received his LLB from Harvard Law School in 1916 and joined the law school faculty in 1917. He left the faculty for a time to join the army during World War I but returned afterwards. At the time he became dean, there were five additional members of the law faculty: Jesse J. M. LaFollette, Merrill I. Schnebly, Hugh E. Willis, Walter Treanor, and James J. Robinson.

McNutt sought to increase both the number of faculty and their salaries in the law school. Low salaries had been a problem across the university for many years, and the university had lost faculty from all departments, including the law school, because of it. In spite of the financial issues, highly regarded faculty were recruited to the school, including Fowler Harper and Bernard L. Gavit. At the same time, the law faculty were becoming more prolific in their scholarship, which McNutt greatly encouraged. Law faculty, including McNutt, regularly published articles in the newly established *Indiana Law Journal*. Robinson authored several casebooks on criminal law and procedure during his time at the law school. Sayre, who was on faculty from 1925 until 1930, published articles in the *Columbia Law Review*, the *Yale Law Journal*, and the *Harvard Law Review* on a variety of legal topics, such as commercial arbitration, landlord-tenant, and family law. McNutt was able to make some improvements for the faculty, but the Great Depression and the conservative nature of the state legislature made it impossible for him to reach his goals. Later, as governor, he remembered this and was sympathetic to the needs of higher education.

After returning from active military duty, McNutt joined the local chapter of the American Legion and traveled the state giving speeches. He held the position of commander of the Indiana American Legion in 1927 and became the national commander of the American Legion in 1928. These experiences whetted McNutt's political appetite, and in 1932, he ran for and was elected governor of Indiana. He remained dean of the law school throughout the campaign, resigning in 1933 just prior to his inauguration. All members of the law school attended the inauguration to support their dean. President Bryan assumed the deanship until a successor could be named.

The period from 1889 to 1933 marked the rebirth of the law school and firmly established its place in the university. The student body grew in numbers and diversity, faculty were added, admission and degree requirements were steadily increased, and graduate degrees were added. Concern was sometimes expressed about the lack of women in the school. While the law school was not actively re-cruiting women, there was no opposition to admitting them. Dean Hepburn stated that he was enthusiastically in favor of women in law and that there was no reason

**FIG. 2.17.** Law students in front of Maxwell Hall. 1930. *Jerome Hall Law Library Archives 010\2014.HIST.30.*

that they could not be as successful as men in the profession. Even so, it would be many years before women were admitted in large numbers.

Even after the law school was given Class A standing in 1923, the growth of the school remained hampered by the lack of educational requirements to practice law in Indiana and by financial constraints. For some, there was no incentive to spend the time and money attending law school when they could become a lawyer without a formal education. In spite of this, the law school produced successful and well-respected graduates. Among them were Sherman Minton, who became a justice of the US Supreme Court; Wendell Willkie, a successful attorney, businessman, and politician, who ran for president on the Republican ticket in 1940; and Hoagy Carmichael, who never really wanted to practice law and instead became one of the most beloved songwriters of the twentieth century.

FIG. 3.1. Law building shortly after construction. Note that Indiana Avenue was a two-way street at this time. October 12, 1957. *IU Archives P0079324.*

# 3 | BUILDING A REPUTATION

*1933–76*

THE OVERWHELMING DEMAND FOR ECONOMIC AND social change swept both President Franklin Roosevelt and Governor Paul McNutt into office in 1932. While the Depression had devastated both financial institutions and a number of universities, under McNutt's tenure as governor, both the law school and Indiana University survived the worst of the era's depredations. Mc-Nutt's time as dean left him acutely aware of the difficulties the university faced, given a lack of state funds for academic programs, salaries, and physical facilities. Governor McNutt would devote much of his four-year term to seeking increased

# BERNARD CAMPBELL GAVIT

Bernard Campbell Gavit, Indiana University
School of Law's seventh dean, was born in
Saginaw, Michigan, but grew up in Hammond,
Indiana, as a member of a prominent family.
Although very short in stature, Gavit was a state
championship track star in high school, which
earned him the lifelong nickname of Bunny
among family and friends. He received his AB
degree at Wabash College, graduating in 1915.
He served in the American Expeditionary Force
during World War I, and following the war,
he returned to school, receiving a JD from the
University of Chicago Law School in 1920. He
then practiced at his family's law firm, Ibach
Gavit Stinson & Gavit, in Hammond, but in
1928, he entered teaching, accepting a position
with the University of Oregon School of Law. The
following year, he was appointed to the faculty at
the Indiana University School of Law. He taught
Wills, Equity, Common Law Actions, Procedure,
Property, Conflict of Laws, Contracts, Torts,
Introduction to Law, Judicial Process, and Legal
Profession. Gavit served as dean from 1933 to
1951, the longest deanship at Indiana to date.

According to a close colleague, when his name
was put forward to succeed Dean Paul McNutt,
Gavit privately expressed reluctance, as the
dean's administrative duties would prevent him
from devoting sufficient time to his real passion:
teaching. Once he decided to accept the deanship,

FIG. SIDEBAR 3.1. Bernard C. Gavit, dean of the law
school, 1933–51. Circa 1933. Photographer: Sinclair
Studio, Bloomington, Indiana.
*IU Archives P0021028.*

appropriations from the General Assembly, as well as assisting the university in
obtaining state and federal funds for badly needed new buildings.

President William Lowe Bryan would remain as acting dean of the law school
for only the 1933 spring semester. In June 1933, the trustees appointed Bernard
Campbell Gavit as dean. Gavit had come to Indiana University in 1929 after
a year of teaching at the University of Oregon School of Law. The law school

however, he quickly devoted himself to elevating the professional stature of Indiana law graduates on two separate fronts: bolstering the requirements for admission to law school and convincing the Indiana General Assembly to strengthen the requirements for the practice of law in the state. He wrote numerous articles and spoke to a wide range of groups to convince the state leaders to raise the standards for admission to the bar.

While Gavit constantly sought out new ways to upgrade both law school admission and graduation standards, he also opposed what he saw as inflexible minimum standards for admission. He wrote that such standards should be "democratic and realistic" and rejected the idea that academic reports should be the ultimate guides about a student's potential success as a lawyer. "I have seen so many risky candidates make the grade, not only in law school but in the practice," he would write in 1950, "that I cannot be sold on the proposition that we cannot afford to take some risks" (Gavit 1950, 27).

He believed that anyone who was interested in becoming a lawyer should study law. When he was asked to advise a student on whether or not to pursue a legal career, Gavit would respond with some variation on a dryly humorous passage from his highly influential book, *Introduction to the Study of the Law*: "Experience teaches me that one called upon to advise another on such a personal and all-important matter as to what one ought to do with his entire life can only accept as a sound formula the following: ascertain (as adroitly as possible, of course) what the victim wants to do and then advise him to do it" (Gavit 1951, 26).

During his scholarly career, Gavit would write over a dozen books and scores of articles. He served in many state and national organizations, including the Indiana State Board of Law Examiners, the Indiana Commission for Uniform Laws, the National Conference of Bar Examiners, and the Association of American Law Schools, to which he was elected secretary in 1941, 1942, and 1946, and president in 1948. In his final speech to the Indiana State Bar Association in 1953, Gavit urged the Indiana Supreme Court to adopt the Federal Rules of Civil Procedure.

In 1951, he stepped down from the deanship after suffering a heart attack at the age of fifty-eight, and he was honored with a portrait from the IU law school alumni in late 1952. Gavit continued to produce books and articles until his death from another heart attack in January 1954, at the age of sixty.

Gavit inherited would see enrollments climb throughout the remainder of the decade. The growing faculty included nationally recognized scholars Walter Treanor, Hugh Willis, James J. Robinson, Robert Brown, Milo Bowman, Alfred Evens, and Fowler Harper as well as librarian Jean Ashman. In the coming years, Gavit would recruit Frank Horack, Jerome Hall, and Leon Wallace to join the faculty.

Dean Gavit wasted no time in beginning a long campaign to raise academic standards. In October 1933, law students with ten hours or more of failing grades would be indefinitely suspended and ineligible for readmission unless the faculty judged that the failures were caused by illness or "other forces over which he had no control" (*Indiana Daily Student*, October 12, 1933, 4). In 1934, the law school increased its admission requirements to three years of undergraduate coursework. Applicants who had not completed a bachelor's degree had to have a 1.6 grade point average (GPA) instead of the 1.2 required of those who had earned a diploma. In order to graduate from law school, students needed to compile a 1.4 GPA on a 3-point scale.

Gavit was equally intent on fighting to raise the standards for admission to the bar, a crusade first taken up by Charles Hepburn and continued by McNutt. By 1923, the Indiana State Bar Association had followed the ABA's lead, adopting a resolution recommending that the state require a law degree as a prerequisite for admission to the bar. In 1932, an amendment to the Indiana Constitution gave the Indiana Supreme Court the power to determine standards for bar admission. In that same year, the court amended its rules to require a state bar examination. Up until this time, any voter of good moral character could be admitted to the bar, but it was not until 1935 that the standards required graduation from an ABA-approved law school.

During the 1930s, as President Roosevelt and Congress introduced a sweeping range of New Deal programs, the university successfully obtained matching grants to add buildings and academic programs. With the completion of Bryan Hall in 1937, the law school, which had been sharing Maxwell Hall with the university's central administration, became its sole occupant. The university allocated $25,000 to renovate Maxwell's basement for use by the law library, and linoleum floors were also installed to cut down on noise.

The renovations came just in time, as law school enrollment continued to grow. The freshman law class of 1936 numbered 110 students following a summer enrollment of 135, the largest in the school's history. A new classroom, big enough to seat 150 students, was created on the second floor of Maxwell Hall in anticipation of an even larger student body.

As busy as they were with the growing number of students, Dean Gavit and his colleagues were incredibly active on both the state and national fronts. Gavit continued to push for reforms in bar admissions on both the Indiana Judicial Council and the State Board of Bar Examiners. New law professor Frank Horack was named as a commissioner to the National Conference on Uniform State Laws and served as a consultant to both the National Marketing Laws Survey and the Indiana State Planning Board. Brown had been a longtime advisor for the State

**FIG. 3.2.** Professor Fowler Harper and Dean Bernard Gavit sing at a Taxi Dance. *1940. Jerome Hall Law Library Archives 010\2014.HIST.33.*

Income Tax Division. Robinson, who would leave Bloomington for Washington, DC, to accept a three-year assignment as a reporter on the Advisory Committee on Federal Laws of Criminal Procedure for the US Supreme Court, was instrumental in the establishment of the IU Institute of Criminal Law Administration and helped establish the State Police Training School. Along with his close involvement with the National Lawyers Guild, Harper chaired the university's Self-Survey Committee, by itself a full-time job, and spent 1939–40 on leave as general counsel to the Federal Security Agency.

Members of the law school faculty were also prolific scholars. Harper wrote on a number of areas of law before he began his pioneering work on tort law, which culminated in both his contributions to the Restatement of Torts and his highly influential treatise on the law of torts. Horack, whose interests ranged from criminal law to land use controls, was one of the leading authorities of his era on

## JEROME HALL

Jerome Hall was born in 1901 and grew up in Chicago, Illinois. He studied at the University of Chicago, earning both his bachelor's in philosophy and his law degree, and was also a Fulbright scholar. Following graduation from law school with honors in 1923, he went on to earn a JurScD at Columbia in 1935 and an SJD from Harvard the same year. Hall spent the majority of his career as professor of law at Indiana University, where he was on faculty from 1939 to 1970, having previously taught at the University of North Dakota, Columbia, and Harvard.

A renowned scholar in criminal law, comparative law, and jurisprudence, with his first book, *Theft, Law and Society*, written in 1935, Hall became one of the first scholars to analyze legal problems through an interdisciplinary approach, pioneering what would become known as the law and society movement. In one of his best known works, *General Principles of Criminal Law*, he developed a single concept of mens rea, a common law principle today regarded as a critical element of proving culpability for a crime. *Readings in Jurisprudence*, first published in 1938, saw multiple editions and was popular both in the United States and in England.

Hall made significant contributions to the global legal community throughout his career. He was an active member of several professional

FIG. SIDEBAR 3.2. Jerome Hall, professor of law, 1939–70. *Jerome Hall Law Library* 002\2013. *FAC.111a.*

legislation and statutory interpretation. Willis, also a legal polymath, wrote over seventy-five articles and books, covering everything from bailments to constitutional law to corporate law.

At least one aspect of their Indiana University experience left law students dissatisfied during this period: their diplomas. In June 1940, law students petitioned the university for a larger certificate of their degree. More precisely, the petition organizations, including serving as chairman and editor of the Modern Legal Philosophy Series from 1940 to 1956 and holding simultaneous presidencies of both the American Society for Political and Legal Philosophy and the American section of the International Association for Philosophy of Law and Social Philosophy in 1965–66.

In 1954, he was one of two Americans approached by the US Department of State to travel to Korea to assist the country in reconstructing their legal system. He spent seven weeks in Korea, then went to Japan for another six weeks, and was then asked to continue on to India for another six weeks, culminating in the Philippines for an additional week. He was named honorary director of the Korean Law Institute in 1955. The State Department came to Hall a second time in 1968, asking him to lecture across Asia as a "leader specialist" in the US State Department's Exchange Program. He advised India on the rewriting of the country's criminal code during this trip.

His international efforts did not end with his involvement with the State Department. He held several prestigious lecturer positions at universities across the globe, including a Fulbright Scholar position at the University of London and Queen's University in Belfast from 1954 to 1955, a Ford Foundation lectureship in 1960 that sent him to Mexico and several countries in South America, a second Fulbright Scholar position in 1961 at Freiburg University, and a Rockefeller Foundation grant to study and lecture on comparative law in Western Europe from 1961 to 1962.

Hall attained the rank of distinguished professor at Indiana University in 1957. On his retirement from IU in 1970, he was invited to join the prestigious Sixty-Five Club at the University of California Hastings College of the Law, a club that encouraged distinguished law professors, upon retirement, to continue their teaching and scholarly pursuits as members of the Hastings faculty. Hall died in 1992. His scholarship continues to have an influence, and his books and articles are still cited regularly in academia today. Indiana University Maurer School of Law's Center for Law, Society, and Culture continues Hall's work in interdisciplinary analysis of legal problems by bringing together scholars from departments and schools across campus to engage in collaborative research and scholarship.

In 2015, Lowell E. Baier (JD; 1964), a former student and research assistant of Hall's, gave a substantial gift to the law school that included naming the law library the Jerome Hall Law Library in honor of his professor and mentor.

requested a diploma similar in size to that received by medical school students, which would be much more suitable for hanging in a practicing attorney's office. By the end of the decade, diplomas from both professional schools would be of matching size.

In 1940, with the approach of the law school's centennial, President Herman B Wells, who had succeeded Bryan in 1937, named a committee of faculty,

**FIG. 3.3.** Law school classroom in Maxwell Hall. February 1941. *IU Archives P0027470.*

administrators, trustees, and alumni to plan an elaborate celebration. The committee invited notable alumni, such as Wendell Willkie and Sherman Minton, along with former dean Paul McNutt, to speak at the ceremonies, which would be capped by a speech from US Supreme Court Chief Justice Charles Evans Hughes. Before arrangements could be finalized, however, the attack on Pearl Harbor occurred. As the country and the university shifted focus to the war effort, and the number of students precipitously dropped, the committee decided to postpone any celebration. In November 1944, a much more subdued commemoration was held.

**FIG. 3.4.** Phi Delta Phi class of 1942 on steps of Maxwell Hall. *Jerome Hall Law Library Archives 010\2014.COMP.47–2.*

## World War II and Its Aftermath, 1941–51

When the war broke out, the law school adopted new rules allowing students to leave midsemester for military service. Law students withdrawing from school for the war who had completed at least ten weeks of a semester would receive full credit for the semester if they were in good standing. Students in their final semester of law school could also receive full credit if they completed only half the semester before entering the service.

**FIG. 3.5.** Hugh Willis, acting dean of the law school, with law student Richard Stack. May 18, 1943. Photographer: Allen Graham. *IU Archives P0039015.*

As World War II deepened, enrollment at the law school plummeted. In 1942–43, forty-eight students were enrolled, and in 1943–44, only twenty-three law students were attending classes. This was the smallest law school enrollment of the twentieth century. By the second semester of 1944, thirty-eight students were enrolled, including ten female students, the first time in the law school's history that female enrollment reached double digits.

Faculty members were also active participants in the war effort. Gavit took a one-year leave to accept the position as general counsel for the War Manpower Commission; Willis, now the senior member of the faculty, served as acting dean during Gavit's absence. Harper also spent the year on leave as an associate member and mediator for industrial disputes on the National War Labor Board, as chairman of the Joint Army and Navy Committee on Welfare and Recreation, and as a legal consultant to the Federal Security Agency. At home, Horack served as director of the university's Office of War Information, charged with advising students on their selective-service and military-training responsibilities.

Soon after Gavit's return to Bloomington, the Indiana Supreme Court proposed that Indiana University take over the independently operated Indianapolis Law School, which was then in danger of losing its ABA accreditation. After discussions with all stakeholders and approval of both boards of trustees, the

FIG. 3.6. Moot Court finals in Maxwell Hall. 1946. *IU Archives P0033898.*

consolidation of the Indianapolis Law School into the Indiana University Law School was announced in July 1944. For the next twenty-five years, Dean Gavit and his successors would serve as the administrator for both schools, and alumni of the Indianapolis school could become alumni of Indiana University on application.

In 1946, Gavit, Harper, and new faculty member Howard Mann signed a petition demanding that the Indiana State Board of Elections follow state law and place the names of Communist Party candidates on the ballot for the fall senatorial election. Governor Ralph Gates and the American Legion pointed to the petition as evidence of subversive activity among the faculty, although all three faculty members had specifically indicated in their petition that they had never been members of the Communist Party nor were they communist sympathizers. Gates requested an investigation by the Indiana University Board of Trustees. Judge Ora L. Wildermuth, chair of the trustees, convened two days of meetings, beginning on September 24, 1946. The board unanimously reported they could find no evidence of communist or subversive teaching.

The controversy was not without repercussions. Harper, who had been cleared by the FBI in late 1946, resigned to manage the Washington, DC, office of the American League for a Free Palestine and joined the Yale Law School faculty

# RALPH FOLLEN FUCHS

Ralph Fuchs was born in 1899 in Saint Louis, Missouri. He earned his undergraduate and JD degrees from Washington University, a doctorate in economics from what is now the Brookings Institute, and a graduate degree in law from Yale. He practiced law privately for one year before joining the faculty at Washington University. During World War II, Fuchs worked for the government, first as administrative head of the Civil Service Commission's Legal Division and then in the solicitor general's office, during which time he argued fourteen cases before the US Supreme Court. In 1946, he became a professor of law at Indiana University and was eventually awarded the title of university professor in honor of his scholarship, teaching, and public service.

Fuchs' scholarly interests were wide ranging, but much of his writing dealt with the then-emerging field of administrative law, in which he was a pioneer. Before coming to IU, he had been an important contributor to one of the most significant pieces of federal legislation affecting administrative law: the Administrative Procedure Act of 1946.

Fuchs was very active in the National Association for the Advancement of Colored People (NAACP) and was appointed to its Committee on Legal Redress in 1949; he also served as faculty advisor to the university chapter of the NAACP. When academic freedom was threatened under the forces of McCarthyism, he worked with the American Association of University Professors (AAUP), both at the campus level and as their national president from 1955 to 1957, to resist this threat and to create a culture of truly meaningful academic freedom. Fuchs's work on behalf of the AAUP also included writing amicus briefs in several Supreme Court cases dealing with the civil rights of scholars. A member of the American Civil Liberties Union since the 1930s, he helped found the Indiana chapter and was the first

chairman of the executive board of the ICLU. Fuchs was also a vital member of the Uniform Law Commission, the American Law Institute, and the Indian Law Institute of New Delhi, spending a year as the Ford Foundation–sponsored director of the joint ALI-ILI in India.

Those who knew Fuchs at every stage of his career all mention his extraordinary personal integrity. His political views were deeply felt, but he never took advantage of his role in the classroom to press his views on students. Throughout his career, he was unfailingly courteous and generous in the support and guidance he offered younger colleagues and students, well beyond his retirement in 1969 up until his death in 1985. The law school awarded Fuchs its Herman Frederic Lieber Award for teaching in 1969 and, in 2001, created the Ralph F. Fuchs Professorship and the Ralph Fuchs Lecture.

FIG. SIDEBAR 3.3. Ralph F. Fuchs, professor of law, 1946–69. October 1947. IU Archives P0048921.

in 1947. When the *Chicago Herald-American* published an article titled "Communism on Campus" and named the three faculty members, Gavit, Mann, and Harper filed a $600,000 lawsuit against the Hearst Corporation for libel, eventually winning a large out-of-court settlement. "Red-baiting" and accusations would also dog law school faculty member Ralph Fuchs as he helped establish the Indiana Civil Liberties Union.

When the war came to an end and soldiers returned to civilian life with GI Bill funding, law school enrollment immediately rebounded. By the 1948–49 school year, 416 students were enrolled. In response to the growing student body, Dean Gavit recruited a number of highly qualified scholars and government attorneys to the faculty. These included Allison Dunham, John Paul Frank, Ralph Fuchs, Austin Clifford, Ben Dutton, Howard Mann, Marsh Wattson, Monrad Paulsen, Franklin Schultz, Val Nolan, Betty LeBus, and Harry Pratter. By the end of the decade, Gavit had truly transformed the law school into one of the finest in the country.

**FIG. 3.7.** Law alumni reunion. Seated at the table are alumnus Sherman Minton (*left*), Governor Henry F. Schricker (*middle*), and former dean Paul McNutt (*right*). June 1950. *IU Archives* P0079325.

FIG. 3.8. Leon Wallace, dean of the law school, 1952–66. October 12, 1957. *IU Archives P0079323.*

By the beginning of 1951, Maxwell Hall had become too small for the faculty and student body. Gavit began talks with the university about a new building, although these were put on hold due to the large number of other campus construction projects. In the meantime, degree requirements were also changing. Law students entering without an undergraduate degree were granted an AB or BS after completion of one year of law school as well as an LLB after an additional two years. Students who had already earned an undergraduate degree were awarded a JD after completion of three years of coursework.

Gavit suffered a heart attack in 1951 and immediately resigned the deanship. President Wells held individual meetings with every law professor about Gavit's successor. Although a number of faculty members suggested Horack and other candidates, Wells appointed Wallace to serve as acting dean for the remainder of the 1951–52 school year.

Leon Harry Wallace was born in Terre Haute, Indiana, in 1904, and earned his undergraduate degree from Indiana University in 1926. After spending four years in San Francisco working for Rand McNally, he returned to Indiana, where he received his law degree from IU in 1933. After graduating, Wallace taught part-time in the law school and worked in his father's Terre Haute law firm. After two years of driving between Terre Haute and Bloomington, Wallace stepped down from teaching to focus solely on the family practice. In 1945, however, he returned to IU to join the law faculty. In 1951, Wallace agreed to serve as the school's acting dean. A year later, on June 2, 1952, he was announced the eighth dean of the Indiana University School of Law.

## Change and Turmoil, 1952–76

Dean Wallace took up planning for a new building where Gavit had left off. After two years of negotiations with the state, Indiana University finally secured

**FIG. 3.9.** Dean Wallace showing law students model of new building. January 7, 1955. *IU Archives P0079337.*

$1,117,908 in December 1954 for the first building specifically designed and built for the law school. In bids announced the following week, Eggers and Higgins of New York was named as the supervising architectural firm, and Huber, Hunt and Nichols of Indianapolis was awarded the general construction contract. On Wednesday, December 29, crews began clearing the site at East Third Street and Indiana Avenue, demolishing the Socony-Vacuum Oil Company service station. In late January, construction began on the new building, which, by completion in August 1956, would cost $1.6 million. An additional $200,000 was allocated for new furniture and equipment. The Mad Monks of Maxwell, as the law students had become known, eagerly anticipated starting classes in their new home. During the final year at Maxwell Hall, the enrollment was 212 students and included 8 female students.

Last-minute delays prevented fall 1956 classes from starting in the new building, but the 275-person student body, fourteen faculty members, and seventy-five thousand library volumes finally occupied the school's new home by the end of

FIG. 3.10. Law building under construction. December 1, 1955. *IU Archives P0079340.*

FACING TOP, FIG. 3.11. Classroom in new law building. 1957. *IU Archives P0079326.*

FACING BOTTOM, FIG. 3.12. Dean Wallace standing in the new moot courtroom. 1957. *Jerome Hall Law Library Archives.*

September 1956. Four classrooms on the first floor would each hold between 75 and 150 students, and the permanent seating and tables in the classrooms required over three thousand holes drilled into the concrete floors. A modern auditorium, accommodating 280, was also built on the first floor for school assemblies, presentations, and courtroom simulations. Four smaller seminar rooms holding 10 to 12 students were located on the second floor. As classes began, Dean Wallace told reporters that the structure was designed to handle anticipated growth for the next fifteen years.

The new building was dedicated in a series of ceremonies from October 31 to November 2, 1957. A number of notable alumni and legal dignitaries attended, including Professor Emeritus James J. Robinson, who had been named to Libya's Supreme Court. Speakers included US Supreme Court Chief Justice Earl Warren; alumnus John S. Hastings, who had recently been confirmed to the US Circuit Court of Appeals for the Seventh Circuit; and Professor Leon Green from the University of Texas.

**FIG. 3.13.** Law school dedication in 1957, moot courtroom. *Standing left to right*: IU President Herman B Wells, former US Supreme Court justice Sherman Minton, Chief Justice of the US Supreme Court Earl Warren, Judge John Hastings of the Seventh Circuit Court of Appeals, and Dean Leon Wallace. *Jerome Hall Law Library Archives 010\2014.HIST.14.*

The law school saw devastating financial cuts in its operating budget during the next ten years. Salaries failed to keep pace with peer institutions, there was no support for summer research or research assistance, the library's collection was falling behind, and other schools were successfully recruiting prominent faculty members. Despite these setbacks, Dean Wallace managed to add Bill Oliver, Ivan Rutledge, Alfred Meyer, and Reed Dickerson, former deputy assistant counsel to the US Department of Defense, to the faculty. In December 1955, Herman C. Krannert, president of Inland Container Corporation of Indianapolis, donated $250,000 for the school's first clinical course, called Legal Techniques, and for scholarships and fellowships. For the next decade, Krannert fellowships were awarded to top law students.

As the law school continued to suffer from budget woes, administrators and faculty explored alternate sources of revenue to supplement state appropriations.

FIG. 3.14. *Indiana Law Journal* board of editors. Note Birch Bayh standing far right. May 14, 1959. *IU Archives P0035977.*

In June 1963, Dean Wallace, Associate Dean Ben Small of the Indianapolis Division, and Executive Director of the IU Foundation William Armstrong announced the inauguration of the Law School Fund, the first formal program designed for annual contributions from alumni and friends of the law school. The recently named IU president, Elvis J. Stahr Jr., himself a former attorney, law professor, and dean, endorsed the campaign, saying "one of my own greatest ambitions for Indiana University is that she have a law school of outstanding and acknowledged quality and reputation" (*Huntington News*, July 22, 1963, 2). One of the goals for the new fund was providing for larger scholarships to attract exceptional students.

In May 1964, the law school announced two additional milestones. Data compiled by the ABA revealed the law school's enrollment of 753 was second in the Big Ten, behind only University of Michigan, and the fourteenth largest enrollment in the country (*Indianapolis Star*, May 27, 1964, 29). It was also in May that the law faculty drafted a report establishing the School of Law Visiting

**FIG. 3.15.** The first Visiting Committee. 1964. *IU Archives P0079353.*

Committee, which would later become known as the Board of Visitors. The report, approved by President Stahr, included the appointment of an initial board of eighteen members that would meet not less than once a year to review a report from the law school on issues such as the curriculum, the *Indiana Law Journal* and other student activities, scholarships, student and faculty recruitment, and graduate placement. Members of the newly formed committee included Earl W. Kintner, Judge Jesse Eschbach, Judge David W. Peck, Judge John S. Hastings, and Indiana Governor Matthew Welsh.

In early 1965, the board of trustees named Dean Wallace to the newly created Charles McGuffey Hepburn Chair of Law. At the same time, he announced his intention to step down from the deanship and return full-time to teaching. At Stahr's request, Wallace agreed to continue as dean until July 1, 1966, to allow sufficient time to find his replacement. A search-and-screen committee chaired by Professor Val Nolan spent the better part of the following year assisting the trustees in finding an ideal candidate, and in May 1966, Stahr announced that William Burnett Harvey would be the next dean.

**FIG. 3.16.** William Burnett Harvey, dean of the law school, 1966–71. *Jerome Hall Law Library Archives 002\2013.FAC.114b.*

William Burnett Harvey was born in Greenville, South Carolina, in 1922 and raised in Erwin, Tennessee. After serving in World War II, he attended Wake Forest College, earning his AB in 1943. He then enrolled at the University of Michigan School of Law, receiving his JD in 1949, and joined the faculty of the Michigan Law School in 1951. In 1962, he took a two-year leave of absence to serve as dean of the University of Ghana Law School, after which he returned to Michigan, remaining there until he was named the ninth dean of the Indiana University School of Law in 1966, the first person to hold the office who was not chosen from within the ranks of the IU faculty.

Clearly understanding that he had been selected to rebuild the law school after a long period of economic decline, Harvey quickly moved to make the admissions criteria for law students more selective and renewed emphasis on excellence in the classroom and scholarship, greatly expanding the faculty with the addition of young teachers with top credentials. In the next five years, Tom Schornhorst, Dan Hopson, Phil Thorpe, Pat Baude, Joe Brodley, Roger Dworkin, Ed Greenebaum,

FIG. 3.17. *Indiana Law Journal* board of editors, 1966–67. April 21, 1967. Photographer: David DeJean. *IU Archives P0071750.*

Bill Popkin, Dan Tarlock, Ed Sherman, Nick White, Morris Arnold, and Henry J. Richardson, the law school's first African American faculty member, would come to IU.

Harvey also enlarged the school's paltry administrative staff, adding a dean of student affairs and a dean for administration and alumni affairs, and created a placement office to assist students with job searches. To give students additional practical experience, he oversaw the development of new clinical programs, including the Federal Prison Clinic, the Clinic on Juvenile Problems, and the Poverty Law Clinic. In 1968, the university's Graduate Council tentatively approved Harvey's proposal for a three-year doctoral program in law and economics. In the same year, the JD degree finally became the standard degree awarded by the law school. Alumni who had previously received an LLB were allowed to convert their degree to a JD.

In early 1968, the law school's Evening Division in Indianapolis gained administrative autonomy and become known as the Indiana University Indianapolis Law School. President Stahr and administrators from both schools believed that the separation would ease enrollment and space problems on both campuses, as a new building was being planned in Indianapolis and a full-time day program was

FIG. 3.18. Law school faculty. 1969. *Jerome Hall Law Library Archives 006\2013.FACG.16.*

to begin in the fall of 1969. Law school enrollment at the Bloomington campus had doubled in the previous five years and stood at 557 in the fall of 1969. Harvey was already concerned over future law library space problems, and the school had rented the house on the southeast corner of Fourth and Dunn Streets for additional offices and classrooms.

The closing years of the 1960s and early 1970s saw the founding of several new student organizations in response to the growing diversity in the student body. In 1969, the Black Law Students Association was organized by twenty-five African American law students, and in the following year, the Association of Women Law Students, later the Women's Law Caucus, was formed. The Legal Services Office opened in early 1971 and was soon renamed Student Legal Services. In 1972, students seeking a stronger voice in law school decision-making formed the Radical Caucus. The Latino Law Students Organization was established in 1972 as well.

Law school faculty members continued to make important contributions in legal scholarship throughout this period. Dickerson built an international reputation as an expert in legislative drafting, writing both the primary treatise and casebook in this area. He also wrote extensively on the developing subjects of products liability and the possible applications of computers in legal research,

## HESS V. INDIANA, 414 US 105 (1973)

In 1970, college campuses across the country were the scenes of massive protests against the Vietnam War. On May 13, 1970, a large group of protesters gathered at Bryan Hall demanding to meet with the university president. City, county, and campus police were there to control the crowds. Undergraduate Gregory Hess came to see what was going on. As police were clearing the streets, Hess yelled, "We'll take the fucking street later!" (or "again"—it is unclear which word was used). The sheriff overheard his words and arrested Hess and a few others for disorderly conduct.

Hearing about this, Professor Tom Schornhorst decided to represent the students in court. As it turned out, only Greg Hess went to trial, where Schornhorst argued that the law was unconstitutional as applied to Hess. The court disagreed and fined Hess twenty-five dollars. Hess could have paid the fine and moved on, but Schornhorst felt there was an important constitutional issue at stake. After appealing to the Indiana Supreme Court to no avail, he asked Professor Pat Baude to assist him. Baude agreed and they set about strategizing how to get the case heard by the US Supreme Court.

They filed an appeal to the US Supreme Court, challenging the constitutionality of the disorderly conduct statute. Surprising everybody, the court summarily reversed the Indiana Supreme Court without briefs or oral argument. Relying on *Brandenburg v. Ohio, 395 US 444* (1969), the court stated about Hess's words that "At best, however, the statement could be taken as counsel for present moderation; at worst, it amounted to nothing more than advocacy of illegal action at some indefinite future time. This is not sufficient to permit the State to punish Hess' speech" (*Hess,* 108). According to Baude, *Hess* clarified that *Brandenburg* was a major change of law, extending First Amendment protection to speech that, while subversive, fell short of inciting immediate unlawful behavior. *Hess v. Indiana* remains an important case today, decided because two law professors would not let the state trample on the constitutional rights of a student.

even before the inception of Lexis and Westlaw. Jack Getman produced a highly influential series of articles and monographs on labor and employment law, which have been frequently cited by scholars, attorneys, and arbitrators. Tarlock was a pioneer and prolific author in the emerging field of environmental law, writing the first casebook as well as teaching one of the first classes in any law school on the critical subject.

The swift changes taking place at the law school were not greeted with universal approval. Despite the significant growth of faculty, curriculum, and students, some alumni did not view Harvey favorably, as they believed that the law school was becoming too liberal. Harvey's staunchest ally in the administration, President Elvis Stahr, had resigned in 1968 to accept the presidency of the National Audubon Society, and the new university administration under President Joseph Sutton was far less supportive of the law school. The Stahr administration had provided the law school with broad economic encouragement, but in 1971–72, the school received only a 2 percent increase to its budget. Dean Harvey submitted his resignation in the fall of 1971 while on leave teaching in Africa. Professor Douglass G. Boshkoff agreed to serve as acting dean from 1971 to 1972 and was appointed to the deanship in 1972.

Douglass G. Boshkoff was born in Buffalo, New York, in 1930. He attended Harvard University, where he earned an AB in 1952 and an LLB in 1955, and returned to Buffalo to practice law from 1955 until 1957, then serving as a teaching fellow at Harvard from 1957 to 1959. He joined the faculty at Wayne State University Law School in 1959 and taught there until joining the law faculty at Indiana University in 1963, after a one-year visiting professorship in Bloomington.

FIG. 3.19. Douglass G. Boshkoff, dean of the law school, 1972–76. Circa 1972. *Jerome Hall Law Library 001\2013.FAC.08–4.*

Boshkoff devoted his five-year tenure to rekindling support for the law school among the university administration, students, members of the state bar, and alumni. He wrote pages of news updates and explanations of curricular changes for every issue of the *Bill of Particulars*, the School of Law Alumni Association's newsletter. He traveled extensively around the state to address various alumni groups, campaigning vigorously for the Law School Fund, which realized increased financial support by 1976. He recruited new faculty members, including Roland Stanger, Jon and Mary-Michelle Hirschoff, Maurice Holland, and Eileen Silverstein, and also named Karen Cutright as assistant dean in 1973. Also during Boshkoff's tenure, a new student-edited journal, *Iustitia*, debuted in the fall of 1973.

**FIG. 3.20.** *Indiana Law Journal* board of editors, 1974–75, posing in front of the house on corner of Fourth and Dunn Streets, where the offices for the journal were located for several years. *Jerome Hall Law Library Archives* 008\2013.JOUR.17.

Boshkoff faced two serious challenges during his deanship. While there had been talk of closing the Bloomington school and moving it to Indianapolis as early as 1962, rumors were reignited after Dean Harvey's resignation. In 1974, Indiana Supreme Court Chief Justice Richard Givan recommended the move, and the university trustees examined a reorganization plan calling for the Bloomington law school to report to the Indianapolis vice president. Boshkoff and the faculty opposed this plan, arguing it would weaken both schools. While the trustees finally decided to shelve the proposal, the recently appointed IU president, John Ryan, convened the Committee of Special Consultants on Legal Education at Indiana University, a "blue ribbon" panel charged with studying the organization of the two schools and making its own assessment. On November 24, 1975, the committee recommended that the university continue to maintain the two schools as separate units despite forceful statements from Indianapolis Dean William F. Harvey advocating for consolidation of the schools in Indianapolis.

In 1974, the Indiana Supreme Court amended Rule Thirteen of the state's Rules for Admission to the Bar to mandate the completion of fifty-four hours of coursework in fourteen different subject areas. The court decided to adopt this measure after the July 1973 bar pass rate dropped to a new low of 75 percent. Dean Boshkoff and the law faculty were concerned that the new rule would hamper curricular development, as it would dictate nearly two-thirds of the coursework for any law student planning to sit for the Indiana Bar. In a detailed study authored by Assistant Dean Karen Cutright and Professor Phillips Cutright of the Sociology Department in 1975, Boshkoff demonstrated through statistical analysis of the July 1973 test takers that there was no support for the rationale behind the amended Rule Thirteen and that no group of courses had any relationship to success or failure on the bar exam. The court and the Board of Law Examiners were unmoved by the study, and Rule Thirteen was applied as a condition of eligibility to take the Indiana bar exam after January 1, 1977.

Boshkoff resigned the deanship in January 1976 to return full-time to teaching and research. The newly appointed vice president for Bloomington, Robert M. O'Neil, formed a search-and-screen committee for the law school's next dean. In the interim, long-time professors Val Nolan and Harry Pratter stepped in as acting deans, Nolan serving the spring and summer of 1976 and Pratter serving until fall of 1977. Nolan and Pratter continued the work of repairing relations with the alumni, both having spent many years prior to their appointments as acting deans traveling across Indiana encouraging enrollment in the law school.

FIG. 4.1. Law school addition. 1986. Photographer: Eggers Group. *Jerome Hall Law Library Archives* *003\2013.BUILD.19.*

# 4 | BECOMING A GLOBAL LAW SCHOOL

## *1976–2017*

I N THE FINAL DECADES OF THE twentieth century, US law schools became multimillion-dollar institutions and often found themselves competing for both students and new ways to define themselves. In addition to struggling to afford faculty, physical facilities, and library collections, law schools facing

FIG. 4.2. Sheldon Jay Plager, dean of the law school, 1977–84. *Jerome Hall Law Library Archives 003\2013.FAC.140.*

the next millennium needed to explore every possible avenue to accommodate revolutionary technologies, evolving teaching methods, clinical opportunities for more practice-ready graduates, and the research requirements of active scholars whose work increasingly extended to foreign and international jurisdictions. Computer technology would transform the entire legal education landscape, and Indiana University School of Law would continue to pursue an unparalleled level of excellence in the broadening study of the law and the emerging global society.

In the self-study report prepared ahead of the 1976 ABA-AALS reaccreditation inspection, School of Law faculty and administrators focused almost exclusively on faculty accomplishments as well as curricular and planning developments. The report, however, contained what was essentially a dire warning for the law school, university, and the state of Indiana: the physical space, and especially the law library, were in critical need of expansion and improvement. The inspection report arrived while Val Nolan was serving as acting dean and a dean search was already under way. The search-and-screen process for a new dean, who would have to answer the considerable challenges the report posed, lasted almost eighteen months. The committee and the school were confident they had found the right person when they announced in January 1977 that the next dean would be Sheldon Jay Plager.

Sheldon Jay Plager served as Indiana University School of Law's eleventh dean from 1977 to 1984. Born in New Jersey in 1931, he received his undergraduate degree from the University of North Carolina in 1952, his JD from the University of Florida in 1958, and an LLM from Columbia Law School in 1961. Prior to arriving at Indiana, Plager taught at the University of Florida from 1958 to 1963 and the University of Illinois from 1964 to 1977. After leaving Indiana, he was a visiting scholar at Stanford University Law School before holding positions in the US Department of Health and Human Services and the US Office of Management

FIG. 4.3. Law school faculty, 1978–79. *Jerome Hall Law Library Archives 006\2013.FACG.17.*

and Budget. Since 1989, he has served as a judge on the US Court of Appeals for the Federal Circuit, assuming senior status in 2000.

In his negotiations with the university, Plager sought IU's renewed financial commitment to the law school, which had struggled financially since the close of Gavit's deanship, and he received a comprehensive package of promises for additional faculty positions, higher faculty salaries, and improved funding for the law library, as well as a pledge to seek state funding for a badly needed building addition and renovation.

Like other top law schools in the nation, IU sought out talented young faculty members with interdisciplinary research interests. Several new professors came with advanced degrees in other subjects in addition to their JDs. Seeking to raise the school's national reputation, Dean Plager emphasized the importance of placing scholarship in highly ranked law journals, thus expanding the law school's visibility. Among these dynamic new faculty were names and faces familiar to

FIG. 4.4. Len Fromm, associate dean for students and alumni affairs, 1979–2013. Len is the only nonalumnus to be inducted into the Academy of Law Alumni Fellows. 1995. *Jerome Hall Law Library Archives 001\2013. FAC.25.*

FIG. 4.5. Members of the Black Law Students Association. April 23, 1980. Photographer: Suzanne Coles. *IU Archives P0079321.*

**FIG. 4.6.** Members of the Women's Law Caucus. April 23, 1980. Photographer: Suzanne Coles. *IU Archives P0079320.*

more recent alumni: John Baker, the law school's first tenured African American faculty member, J. William Hicks, Craig Bradley, Bryant Garth, Julia Lamber, Alex Tanford, Terry Bethel, Merritt Fox, Ann Gellis, Bob Heidt, Dan Conkle, and Richard Lazarus. In the second year of his tenure, Plager also named Leonard D. Fromm as the school's new dean of students. For his colleagues and generations of students, Len Fromm was an integral ingredient of the law school's heart and soul, from his arrival in 1979 until his passing in 2013.

The fall of 1980 saw the beginning of center-based programs. Citing the explosion of sports litigation at both amateur and professional levels, the Lilly Endowment made a grant of $85,000 for the development and support of the Center for

FIG. 4.7. Ground-breaking for the law school addition. *Pictured left to right:* Dean Sheldon J. Plager, President John Ryan, and Vice President Kenneth Gros Louis. November 22, 1982. *Jerome Hall Law Library Archives 002\2013.BUILD.9–2.*

Law and Sports. The center's inaugural director, Ronald Waicukauski, led in the organization of several national conferences and edited a volume of critical essays on the intersection of athletics and the law.

In 1980, President John Ryan and the university made good on the promise to prioritize the law school's building addition. With lobbying from Val Nolan, who served as acting dean while Plager was on leave for a semester, the Indiana Higher Education Commission granted $145,000 for site plans and schematics, and Plager announced that Professor Craig Bradley would chair the building committee. The Indiana General Assembly approved finances for the project in two phases, in 1981 and in 1984. Ground-breaking for the $12.6 million project took place on November 22, 1982, commencing three-and-one-half years of site preparation, construction, and renovation.

Perhaps the strangest and most publicized phenomenon attending the law school construction project was the Save the Trees movement, which reached its

FIG. 4.8. Save the Trees protesters tying ribbons around trees they fear will be lost in the law school construction. 1982. *Jerome Hall Law Library Archives 002\2013.BUILD.6.*

peak during the 1982 spring semester. As architects were still submitting preliminary drafts of the library addition on the east side of the law building, members of the university community and the public began voicing increasingly alarmed concern over the possible destruction of old-growth trees in Dunn's Woods. Letters to the editor in the Bloomington *Herald-Telephone* and the *Indiana Daily Student* lamented the loss of the entire forested area of the Old Crescent, with one writer fearing the law school construction would call for the removal of the Well House! Petitions circulated calling for alterations to the addition plans, one of which was signed by composer-conductor Leonard Bernstein, who was an artist in residence at the IU School of Music in 1982. Save the Trees culminated in a ceremony during which yellow and green ribbons were tied around trees that protestors believed would be removed, a number of which had actually been planted after the 1956 completion of the law building. In reality, only three trees were lost, none of which were old-growth trees from Dunn's Woods.

During the construction and renovation, students, faculty, and the library occupied separate buildings on campus. The seats and tables were moved from the law school building to the Student Building, where classes were held during the fall, spring, and summer semesters of the 1984–85 school year. The faculty moved

**FIG. 4.9.** Law students holding sign thanking the state legislature for funding the addition. Law students were an integral part of the campaign to obtain funding for the construction project. 1984. *Jerome Hall Law Library Archives 002\2013.BUILD.9–6.*

**FIG. 4.10.** Morris Sheppard "Buzz" Arnold, dean of the law school in 1985. *Jerome Hall Law Library Archives 001\2013.FAC.89b.*

into Memorial Hall for the year, while the library moved into the new addition after final exams in December 1984.

It was also in 1984 that Plager resigned his deanship to first pursue a research leave and then return to teaching. Associate Dean Maurice Holland served as acting dean, and a search-and-screen committee, headed by Professor Bill Hicks, was appointed. Just as renovations to classrooms and faculty offices were coming to a close in the summer of 1985, former IU School of Law professor Morris Arnold was appointed to the deanship.

Morris Sheppard Arnold served as Indiana University School of Law's twelfth dean. Born in Texarkana, Texas, in 1941 and educated at the Exeter Academy in New Hampshire, he spent two years at Yale before graduating with a BS from the University of Arkansas in 1965. He then attended the University of Arkansas Law School, where he received his LLB in 1968, after which he received an LLM in 1969 and doctor of juridical science (SJD) in 1971 from Harvard Law School. Arnold joined the faculty at Indiana in 1971, remaining until 1977, when he accepted a

FIG. 4.11. US Supreme Court Chief Justice William Rehnquist and President John Ryan at the dedication ceremony for the addition. September 12, 1986. *Jerome Hall Law Library Archives 009\2014.BUILD.1–35.*

FIG. 4.12. Bryant G. Garth, dean of the law school, 1987–90. *Jerome Hall Law Library Archives 002\2013.FAC.109a.*

position at the University of Pennsylvania Law School. In 1981, he joined the faculty at the University of Arkansas School of Law, remaining there until 1984. In 1985, Arnold returned to Indiana University to become dean of the law school; however, soon after arriving at Indiana, Arnold was nominated, and ultimately confirmed, to become a judge of the US District Court for the Western District of Arkansas. In 1992, he was appointed to the US Court of Appeals for the Eighth Circuit and assumed senior status in 2006.

During the six months of his deanship, Arnold commenced negotiations with the university for the computerization of the law school. During the following year, all faculty members, administrators, and support staff would have personal computers in their offices. The package Arnold negotiated also included a computer center for student word processing and online-resource training in the law library. In the midst of the renovations, the faculty added fresh new talent to their ranks. Joining the faculty were alumna Lauren Robel; Steve Conrad; Jeff Stake; John Scanlan, who took over the Law and Sports Center; and Joe Hoffmann, a former clerk to US Supreme Court Justice William Rehnquist.

On his confirmation to the US District Court, Dean Arnold resigned in December 1985. Associate Dean Maurice Holland once again stepped in as acting dean, and Hicks returned as head of a new search-and-screen committee. Holland resigned in the late spring of 1986 to assume the deanship at the University of Oregon School of Law, at which time Bryant G. Garth was named acting dean. The summer of 1986 also saw the completion of construction and renovations, with all personnel finally back in their permanent offices. A dedication ceremony for the addition was held September 12, 1986, at the IU Auditorium. IU President John Ryan and Indiana Governor Robert D. Orr gave speeches, and US Supreme Court

Justice William Rehnquist presented a dedicatory address, "The Legal Profession Today," just two weeks prior to being sworn in as chief justice. The following semester, in the spring of 1987, Garth was appointed to the deanship.

Bryant Geoffrey Garth was the school's thirteenth dean, serving from 1987 to 1990. Born in San Diego, California, in 1949, he received his BA from Yale in 1972, his JD from Stanford in 1975, and his PhD from the European University Institute in 1979. He joined the faculty at Indiana in 1979, remaining until 1990, when he became director of the American Bar Foundation, where he would stay until 2004. In 2005, Garth became dean of the Southwestern School of Law, a position he held until 2012, when he joined the faculty of the UC Irvine School of Law.

By the mid-1980s, the needs of the modern law school had far outstripped decreasing state funds, and one of Garth's priorities was to expand resources for financial support. By focusing on alumni giving, Garth was able to establish a general endowment of $500,000. During this time, the law school also received $1.5 million as a bequest from the estate of a former president of the IU Law Alumni Association, Roscoe O'Byrne, and his wife, Estella. His deanship also saw the birth and development of a number of new organizations. Garth founded the Law and Society Center in 1987 to sponsor and foster interdisciplinary research at the university, an area of importance for the law school since the pioneering work of Jerome Hall.

In April 1987, the Community Legal Clinic was organized through a federal grant and would eventually be led in 1989 by returning alumnus Earl Singleton. In 1989, the Protective Order Project was established with the assistance of Lauren Robel. Both programs helped enhance clinical opportunities for students as well as contribute to the public interest legal needs of the community. In support of the latter function, law students Colleen Cotter, Nan Nash, Elizabeth Thompson, and Jacqueline Zydeck formed the Public Interest Law Foundation in January 1988, with faculty assistance by Pat Baude and David Medine.

The faculty and student body continued to grow during Garth's tenure. By April 1989, applications had increased by 32 percent. A new pool of scholarly talent included faculty members Kevin Brown, Gene Shreve, Don Gjerdingen, and Fred Cate, who would become the founding director of IU's Center for Applied Cybersecurity Research in 2003 and vice president for research at IU in 2015. Also joining the faculty in 1987 was Thomas Ehrlich, who was named the fifteenth president of Indiana University that year. In the spring of 1990, Garth stepped down to become the director of the American Bar Foundation, and Terry Bethel, associate dean and professor since 1979, was appointed acting dean. A search-and-screen

FIG. 4.13. *Indiana Law Journal* board of editors, 1988–89. *Jerome Hall Law Library Archives 008\2013.JOUR.19.*

FIG. 4.14. Alfred C. Aman Jr., dean of the law school, 1991–2002. 1995. Photographer: Annalese Poorman. *Jerome Hall Law Library Archives 001\2013.FAC.03.*

committee was formed, and in the spring of 1991, came the announcement that Alfred Aman would become the law school's fourteenth dean and the third dean not to have previously served on the faculty.

Alfred C. Aman Jr. was born in 1945 in Rochester, New York. He received his BA from the University of Rochester in 1967 and his JD in 1970 from the University of Chicago Law School, where he served as executive editor of the University of Chicago Law Review. From 1970 to 1972, Aman served as a clerk to Elbert P. Tuttle on the US Court of Appeals for the Fifth Circuit. He then spent five years as attorney with the firm of Sutherland Asbill & Brennan, before joining the faculty of the Cornell Law School in 1977, where he taught until coming to Indiana.

Aman immediately set about expanding the law school's focus to encompass a global approach to teaching, research, and scholarship, and created partnerships with European scholars, including visiting professors Paul Craig, professor of English law from the University of Oxford; Elizabeth Zoller, professor of public law in the law school at the University of Paris II (Panthéon-Assas); Jost Delbrück, dean of the faculty of laws, president, and rector of the University of Kiel; and Yvonne Cripps, who had previously served as an advisor on intellectual property law and biotechnology to the House of Lords. In addition, Aman sought and received major contributions to establish fully funded professorships and six fellowships to foster new avenues of faculty research.

The new funding sources and a greater commitment to diversity and excellence led to the appointment of an entire cadre of talented scholars, including Ken Dau-Schmidt; Rob Fischman; Aviva Orenstein; Alysa Rollock, the law school's first female African American professor; Susan Williams; David Williams; Hannah Buxbaum; David Fidler; Dawn Johnsen; Marshall Leaffer; John Applegate; Amy Applegate; Charlie Geyh; Jeanine Bell, who would become the school's first female tenured African American professor; Jim Barnes, the former dean of the

## GLOBAL OPPORTUNITIES FOR STUDENTS

The Maurer School of Law has long embraced the value of global experiences for its graduates. As early as 1986, it recognized the benefit of foreign study to students when it joined the London Law Consortium, enabling students to attend classes in London for a semester. Today, students have numerous opportunities to study and work abroad. Through the school's partnership with the University of San Diego, students can study in London and Paris during the summer. There are additional opportunities for summer and semester study abroad through partnerships and exchange programs with foreign law schools in France, Germany, Italy, Spain, the Netherlands, Ireland, Hungary, Poland, China, Hong Kong, India, Australia, New Zealand, and Mexico.

The Milton Stewart Fellows Overseas Externship Program gives students the opportunity to work abroad during the summer. This unique and prestigious program began in 2010 through the generosity of Milton (JD; 1971) and Judi Stewart. Selected fellows spend the summer working around the globe in a variety of settings, including corporations, nongovernmental organizations, and law firms. As of 2018, over 125 Maurer students have been selected as Stewart Fellows. The program is administered through the Milt and Judi Stewart Center on the Global Legal Profession. Founded in 2009, the center was named for Milt and Judi Stewart in October 2016, following their generous $7.7 million estate gift, endowing the center and a professorship.

FIG. SIDEBAR 4.1. Milton (JD; 1971) and Judi Stewart. The Milt and Judi Stewart Center on the Global Legal Profession was named in honor of their generous support to the center and the Stewart Fellows. October 2016. *Photo courtesy of IU Foundation.*

IU School of Public and Environmental Affairs; and Luis Fuentes-Rohwer, the school's first Latino professor.

In 1992, Aman announced the inauguration of the *Indiana Journal of Global Legal Studies*, which would include annual symposia presented by some of the world's most preeminent legal scholars. During the same year, the school also took over editorial responsibilities for the *Federal Communications Law Journal*, providing, along with the *Indiana Law Journal*, expanded opportunities for journal experience for nearly one-third of the school's second-year students. Aman also oversaw the creation of the school's SJD program and the considerable expansion of the LLM program, both of which would flourish through partnerships with a number of foreign and international law schools.

Like other American law school deans, Aman and his successors were becoming increasingly concerned with the relatively new phenomenon of the *U.S. News*

**FIG. 4.15.** The trial of Richard III, held in the moot courtroom, October 26, 1996. *On the bench from left to right:* Indiana Supreme Court Chief Justice Randall Shepard, US Supreme Court Chief Justice William Rehnquist, and Professor Susan Williams. At the podium is James Fitzpatrick (JD; 1959). *Jerome Hall Law Library Archives 028\2016.EVENT.205–36.*

**FIG. 4.16.** The court-martial of George Armstrong Custer, held in the moot courtroom, September 18, 1998. *On the bench from left to right:* Indiana Supreme Court Justice Frank Sullivan Jr. (JD; 1982), US Supreme Court Justice Ruth Bader Ginsburg, and Professor David Williams. Photographer: Nick Judy. *Jerome Hall Law Library Archives 020\2015.EVENT.131–143.*

*& World Report* annual rankings of law schools. First published in 1987, the rankings would become perhaps the most influential tool prospective law students would use in their decision-making, despite severe criticism of the publication and its methodology by both law school administrators and the ABA. The ABA, in fact, received so many complaints from the academy that, by 1994, its official position was to denounce the rankings. Aman pointed out that one of the problems with the rankings was that "a survey like this has the tendency to overweigh the past. Reputations in the academic world have a way of living long past the reasons that create those reputations" (Magan 1994, 8). He nevertheless conceded that the rankings were definitely influencing recruiting.

Of the many notable speakers, presentations, and special programs during Aman's deanship, the most remarkable were a pair of mock trials that garnered national coverage. On October 26, 1996, US Supreme Court Chief Justice William Rehnquist returned to Bloomington to join Indiana Supreme Court Chief Justice Randall Shepard and Professor Susan Williams to judge the trial of the British

## LAUREN K. ROBEL

Lauren Robel was born in Omaha, Nebraska, in 1953. Due to her father's career in the US Air Force, she lived in multiple locations before graduating from high school, finally settling in Montgomery, Alabama. Robel earned a BA degree in English literature from Auburn University in 1978, before arriving in Bloomington to attend law school in 1980. Robel received her JD, summa cum laude, from Indiana University School of Law in 1983.

After graduation, she clerked for Judge Jesse Eschbach at the US Court of Appeals for the Seventh Circuit in Chicago and returned Bloomington in 1985 when she was appointed as an assistant professor at IU. A highly regarded and popular teacher, Robel earned acclaim for her scholarship on federal procedure and the federal courts. She took on a number of pro bono efforts, often working with students, as appointed counsel in criminal, habeas, and civil rights cases for the Seventh Circuit Court of Appeals and spearheading the law school's Protective Order Project. She was promoted to associate professor in 1987 and professor of law in 1990.

The following year Robel was appointed associate dean of the law school, a position she held until she was named dean in 2003 (she was interim dean in 2002). While associate dean, in 2000, she was honored as the first Val Nolan Chair in Law, endowed by Mickey Maurer (JD; 1967) and named for his favorite professor.

Under Robel's leadership, the School of Law rose in national stature to be regarded as one of the top public law schools in the country. During her tenure, new centers and clinics were created, and talented new faculty were hired. A highlight of her deanship was the naming of the law school in 2008, made possible by the generosity of alumnus Michael S. "Mickey" Maurer (JD; 1967) and his wife, Janie. In January 2011, Robel was elected as the president-elect of the Association of American Law Schools and served a one-year term as AALS president beginning in January 2012.

Robel found time to give back to the Bloomington community. She served as chair of the Bloomington Human Rights Commission from 1986 to 1991; was president for two years and then member of the Habitat for Humanity of Monroe County Board of Directors; and was cochair of the United Way Campaign for Indiana University from 2005 to 2007.

In late 2011, it was announced that Robel would be the interim provost for the Bloomington campus, and in 2012, she was named provost of Indiana University Bloomington and executive vice president of Indiana University. Among her major accomplishments to date has been implementing the recommendations of the New Academic Directions report, which called for several new schools and interdisciplinary programs, including global, online, and student success initiatives.

FIG. SIDEBAR 4.2. Lauren K. Robel, dean of the law school, 2003–12. 2002. *Jerome Hall Law Library Archives* 001\2013.FAC.56a.

king Richard III for the murders of his nephews. Participating in the trial were James Fitzpatrick (JD; 1959), John Walda (JD; 1975), and students Dennis Long and Paige Porter. Fred Cate and David Williams edited a record of the proceedings, which were held in the Sherman Minton Moot Courtroom. On September 18, 1998, the court-martial of George Armstrong Custer was held in the moot courtroom, judged by US Supreme Court Justice Ruth Bader Ginsburg, Indiana Supreme Court Justice Frank Sullivan Jr. (JD; 1982), and Professor David Williams. Participating in the trial were Kathleen Buck (JD; 1973), Robert Long (JD; 1971), and law students Damon Leichty and Azin Lofti. Cate, Williams, and Dennis Long edited the publication of the proceedings.

Aman stepped down from the deanship in 2002 to return to teaching and research. In 2007, he accepted the deanship at Suffolk University School of Law in Boston but returned to Indiana in 2009, where he became the Roscoe C. O'Byrne Professor of Law. A prolific scholar, Aman has published numerous books and articles on administrative law, international law, and globalization. Associate Dean Lauren Robel was appointed acting dean, and after a search-and-screen committee was formed, she was appointed as the school's fifteenth dean and first female dean in 2003.

## Transformative Centers and Transformational Gifts

Dean Robel directed a level of growth and progress unprecedented in the school's history. Sections of the school's second and third floor, formerly occupied by the law library, were renovated to add new classrooms and seminar spaces, faculty offices, student areas, and administrative offices, as well as a faculty conference room. In 2006, the school developed a new strategic plan, setting out a course for the future. This plan included the expansion of the school into the newly constructed Lewis Building on the opposite corner of Indiana Avenue and Fourth Street to house the school's burgeoning clinical programs, and the Development and Alumni Affairs Building on Third Street, named for former assistant dean Art Lotz. In September 2006, the Lewis Building also became the home to the new Conservation Law Clinic, established in partnership with the Conservation Law Center and headed by the center's president, Clinical Professor William Weeks.

In the spring of 2007, alums David Elmore (JD; 1958) and D. G. Elmore Jr. (JD; 1984) made a $3 million gift to fund scholarships for Entrepreneurship Law Clinic students, joint JD/MBA candidates, and students demonstrating a strong interest in business law. In recognition of this significant gift, the law school formally named the Elmore Entrepreneurship Law Clinic during a well-attended

FIG. 4.17. Law school faculty, 2006–7. *Jerome Hall Law Library Archives 006\2013.FACG.12–2.*

ceremony in October 2007. The fall of 2007 also saw the inauguration of the Center for Constitutional Democracy, founded by Professor David Williams. The center, which would establish projects in Liberia, Burma, and Central Asia, was created to build legal institutions promoting peace, justice, and democracy in recently war-torn countries, and it is one of the only centers in the world engaged in constitutional-design consulting.

In December 2007, the Lilly Endowment provided a $25 million grant to enable the school to attract and retain extraordinary scholars and to help establish the school as one of the finest public university law schools in the country. "This gift will help us position our School of Law at the forefront of legal education by enabling the school to vigorously compete for the very best faculty and students from around the globe," said IU President Michael McRobbie (IU News Bureau, December 12, 2007). Among the new and accomplished faculty who would join the law school during Robel's deanship were Bill Henderson, Christiana Ochoa,

FIG. 4.18. President McRobbie announcing renaming the school to the Maurer School of Law in honor of the generous gift from Mickey and Janie Maurer. *From left to right:* President Michael McRobbie, Michael S. "Mickey" Maurer (JD; 1967), Janie Maurer, and Dean Lauren Robel (JD; 1983). December 4, 2008. Photographer: Chris Meyer. *Maurer School of Law Photo Archive Maurer law 120408CM172.*

Ajay Mehrotra, Leandra Lederman, Tim Waters, Carwina Weng, Donna Nagy, Jody Madeira, Brian Broughman, Jay Krishnan, Ryan Scott, Deborah Widiss, Dan Cole, and IU alumni Mark Janis and Mark Need.

Robel also spearheaded a major change in the first-year curriculum. Citing the law school's partnership in a three-year project on law school curricula, sponsored by the Stanford Law School and the Carnegie Foundation for the Advancement of Teaching following the 2007 publication of Carnegie's *Educating Lawyers: Preparation for the Profession of Law,* Robel announced the new Legal Professions class, which would focus more explicitly on helping students develop a sense of professional identity and purpose. The class was taught for the first time in the spring of 2008. In the same year, the Family and Mediation Clinic, now headed by Amy Applegate, was named for Judge Viola Taliaferro (JD; 1977).

On December 4, 2008, McRobbie formally announced the naming of the Indiana University School of Law–Bloomington in honor of Indianapolis business and community leader Michael S. "Mickey" Maurer (JD; 1967). The gift of $35

# MICHAEL S. "MICKEY" MAURER

An Indianapolis native, Mickey Maurer graduated from North Central High School and received a bachelor's degree in accounting from University of Colorado. He returned to Indiana for law school, earning a JD in 1967. After graduation, Maurer moved to New York City, where he spent two years working at a Wall Street law firm before returning to Indianapolis to practice law at the firm of Maurer, Rifkin & Hill. He also launched a number of successful entrepreneurial ventures in communications and entertainment, including cable television systems in Indiana and Michigan, a group of radio stations, film production, and print publications.

Maurer serves as chairman of the board of IBJ Corporation, which owns and publishes the *Indianapolis Business Journal*, *Court and Commercial Record*, and the *Indiana Lawyer*. Additionally he serves as chairman of the board of directors of the National Bank of Indianapolis. In 2001, he established Mickey's Camp, a charitable endeavor that has raised more than $3 million for central Indiana charities. In 2005, he was named president of the Indiana Economic Development Corporation and in 2006 was appointed Indiana secretary of commerce by Governor Mitch Daniels. Maurer is a published contributor to the *New York Times* crossword puzzle and has authored three books: *Water Colors* (2003), *19 Stars of Indiana–Exceptional Hoosier Women* (2009), and *19 Stars of Indiana– Exceptional Hoosier Men* (2010).

A devoted supporter of Indiana University and the School of Law, Maurer chaired the law school's first and highly successful capital campaign during the 1990s. His service, loyalty, and leadership earned him a place in the Academy of Law Alumni Fellows in 1996. In 2000, he and his wife, Janie, endowed the Val Nolan Chair in Law, in honor of his favorite professor. Maurer received the IU Distinguished Alumni Service Award in

2001, and in 2007, he received the IU Foundation President's Medal for his outstanding and sustained support of the IU Foundation and the university. He was awarded an honorary doctor of humane letters degree from Indiana University in 2016.

On December 4, 2008, President Michael A. McRobbie announced that the IU Law School would be renamed the Michael Maurer School of Law in recognition of Maurer's longtime support for the school and his $35 million gift for law student scholarships. "This gift is special for me because it is an opportunity to say thank you to an institution that made possible the success I have enjoyed in my legal and business career, the IU School of Law in Bloomington," Maurer said. "Janie and I make this contribution to the Law School with confidence in Lauren Robel, who has served our school so well. We fully expect under Dean Robel's guidance that this school will be recognized as an elite institution and assuredly one of the finest public law schools in the nation" (IU News Bureau Press Release, December 4, 2008).

FIG. SIDEBAR 4.3. Mickey Maurer (JD; 1967) speaking at the naming announcement. December 4, 2008. Photographer: Chris Meyer. *Maurer School of Law Photo Archive Maurer law 120408CM401.*

million from Maurer and his wife, Janie, was designated for law student scholarships. In his statement, McRobbie said, "This exceptional gift builds on the Law School's foundation of excellence. It will enable Indiana University to continue to attract top law students and to provide them with the essential knowledge and practical training vital in today's complex legal environments" (IU News Bureau Press Release, December 4, 2008). Robel added, "It is a commitment that resonates through all the members of the school's family, from alumni and faculty to administrators and students. I am confident that this gift will help us secure our place in the highest echelon of law schools nationwide" (IU News Bureau Press Release, December 4, 2008). At the time of the renaming, the Maurer School of Law was home to 738 law students, fifty-nine faculty members, and fourteen administrators.

In August 2009, Robel announced the launching of Maurer's new Center on the Global Legal Profession, which would focus on the challenges lawyers faced around the world and would assist current and future attorneys in their understanding of international legal systems. In announcing the inception of the center, its first director, Professor Bill Henderson, stated, "This is the first time we will have legal academics step back and look at the global legal industry as a whole and acknowledge patterns that have evolved over the last few decades" (IU News Bureau Press Release, August 11, 2009). The launch was also announced in New Delhi, India, where a conference on globalization and the practice of law was sponsored by Maurer and the Jindal Global Law School. This was the beginning of a robust partnership with Jindal, which continued under the center's subsequent director, Professor Jay Krishnan.

A very different kind of partnership was established at Maurer Law in the summer of 2010, when US Court of Appeals for the Seventh Circuit Judge David F. Hamilton announced plans to relocate his chambers to the school. Hamilton, an emeritus member of the school's Board of Visitors and a member of the board of directors for the Center for Constitutional Democracy, moved his chambers from Indianapolis to Maurer in order to give law students exposure to the workings of the judicial system and to explore new learning opportunities with the school. Renovations to accommodate Judge Hamilton's chambers on the second floor of the building required relocation of the school's mock trial room and the law library's student computer lab and were completed by the end of 2010.

In May 2011, Maurer Law launched the Center for Intellectual Property Research, directed by Professor Mark Janis, who said that the center's purpose would be to support the study of all aspects of intellectual property law and related fields, including patent, trademark and unfair competition, copyright, and information policy. "Every lawyer needs to understand how technology intersects

**FIG. 4.19.** Austen L. Parrish, dean of the law school, 2014–. February 2018. Photographer: Ann Schertz. *Maurer School of Law Photo Archive.*

with the law," Janis explained, "and in no area is that intersection more salient than in intellectual property law. The center will promote a dialogue on intellectual property law among scholars, judges, policymakers, practitioners and students" (IU News Bureau Press Release, May 5, 2011). The center would also publish *IP Theory,* an online peer-reviewed forum for essays, opinion pieces, and literature reviews. The year 2011 also saw the inauguration of another online journal, the *Indiana Journal of Law and Social Equality,* which would serve as an interdisciplinary academic forum on society's understanding of legal and policy issues concerning race, religion, gender, and class for scholars, practitioners, policy makers, and students.

In December 2011, the IU Board of Trustees announced Robel's appointment as interim provost for the Bloomington campus and appointed Associate Dean Hannah Buxbaum, who had joined the faculty in 1997, as Maurer's acting dean. During Buxbaum's interim deanship, four new and talented teachers joined the faculty: Timothy Lovelace, Michael Mattioli, Victor Quintanilla, and Steve Sanders. A dean search committee was appointed in 2012, chaired by Professor John Applegate, who had been appointed IU vice president for planning and policy in July 2008. In the late fall of 2013, the IU Board of Trustees appointed Austen L. Parrish as the sixteenth dean of the Maurer School of Law. Buxbaum returned to teaching and, in July 2018, became Indiana University's vice president for international affairs.

Austen L. Parrish became dean in January 2014. Born in Vancouver, British Columbia, in 1972, Parrish received his BA in 1994 from the University of Washington and his JD in 1997 from Columbia University. After law school, he became an associate at the Los Angeles offices of O'Melveny & Myers, where he remained until joining the faculty at Southwestern Law School in 2002. In addition to rising to the rank of professor of law at Southwestern, Parrish served as vice dean for academic affairs from 2008 to 2012 and interim dean and chief executive officer from 2012 to 2013.

During his candidate presentations to Maurer faculty and students, Parrish set forth his goals of developing new strategies for the school's long-term prosperity. His plans were set against a backdrop of declining law school applications and waning employment of new attorneys, both a result of the 2008 market crash and recession. To this end, Parrish immediately began establishing partnerships with a number of prestigious undergraduate institutions throughout the country to create new pathways for prospective law students. Scholarship and mentorship programs were formed with, among others, DePauw University, Princeton University, Iowa State College of Engineering, Rose-Hulman Institute of Technology, and Albion, Coe, Dartmouth, Grinnell, Kenyon, Vassar, and Wabash colleges.

Expanding Maurer's international mission, Parrish sought additional partnerships with foreign law schools on four continents, visiting schools around the world to cement new exchange programs, including King Saud Law School, Peking University Law School in Beijing, Università Bocconi (Milan), and Leiden University in the Netherlands. In addition, a scholarship partnership for Mexican LLM students was established with FUNED, La Fundación Mexicana para la Educación, la Tecnología, y la Ciencia. Parrish also opened discussions at home on the IU campus with the College of Arts and Sciences, Kelley School of Business, Jacobs School of Music, School of Global and International Studies, and School of Public and Environmental Affairs to promote the idea of bringing IU's finest undergraduates to Maurer. To underwrite his new programs and initiatives, he spearheaded the law school's capital campaign program with the goal of raising $60 million in gifts and contributions.

During his deanship, Parrish and Maurer Law have expanded the range of domestic externships available, from county prosecutors' offices to nonprofit organizations and the judiciary; offered hands-on projects that would enable students to provide legal assistance to inmates, immigrants, tenants, victims of domestic violence, and members of the LGBT community; and created new initiatives to help students find their first jobs through an innovative bridge-to-practice series. Parrish also reached out to younger alumni groups around the United States to shore up mentoring programs and foster networking events in major cities around the country. Back at Maurer Law, he took numerous steps to improve engagement with and by law students, including extended open-door hours for all administrative offices and a monthly Coffee and Cookies with the Dean, held in the lobby of the law library.

**FIG. 4.20.** President McRobbie with Lowell E. Baier (JD; 1964) at the ceremony renaming the building Baier Hall in honor of his generous gift. The law library was renamed the Jerome Hall Law Library at the same ceremony in honor of Baier's favorite professor. May 8, 2015. Photographer: Deborah W. Conkle. *Jerome Hall Law Library Archives 031\2017.EVENT.6–41.*

On May 8, 2015, the Maurer School of Law held a dedication ceremony to honor the many contributions of alumnus and entrepreneur Lowell Baier. In recognition of his support and a generous estate gift of $20 million, the law school building was renamed Baier Hall, and the law library was renamed the Jerome Hall Law Library, in honor of the faculty member who had most inspired Baier both in and out of the classroom.

In 2015, Maurer Law launched the online *Indiana Journal of Constitutional Design*. Published through the Center for Constitutional Democracy, this was the first journal devoted specifically to the emerging field of constitutional design. Articles examine the ways in which basic legal ordering (the law that creates the fundamental power structures of a given country) shapes and is shaped by political, economic, and cultural conditions. This online journal publishes a range of different materials, including not only traditional articles and student notes, but also taxonomies of design options on particular subjects, explorations of specific

## LOWELL E. BAIER

Lowell E. Baier was born in 1940 in Chicago, Illinois. He received his BA in economics and political science from Valparaiso University in 1961 and his JD from the Indiana University School of Law in 1964. He was also honored by his alma mater with an LLD in 2010 and a doctor of humane letters (LHD) in 2015. After graduation, Baier practiced law in Washington, DC, a city he'd grown to love when, in 1956, his congressman, Charles A. Halleck, selected him as a page in the US House of Representatives. During his early years in the practice of law, he formed Baier Properties, Inc., a Bethesda, Maryland, based developer of warehouses, residential properties, and award-winning office buildings and shopping centers.

Baier's lifelong passion for protecting the country's natural resources and wildlife conservation began during his childhood while he was being raised on a farm in northern Indiana and spending time on his grandfather's homestead ranch in Montana. In the early 1970s, he was one of the original fourteen founders of the Wild Sheep Foundation, which has funded over $2.4 million annually to reestablish the historical habitat of the four species of wild sheep in North America. The success of this effort led to similar programs in both Russia and Mongolia.

FIG. SIDEBAR 4.4  Lowell E. Baier at the 2014 Academy of Law Alumni Fellows ceremony upon the occasion of his induction. April 11, 2014. Photographer: Ann Schertz. *Jerome Hall Law Library Archives 035\2014.ALAF.1–10.*

drafting issues in particular countries, and reflections by those with experience in constitutional drafting and design.

During the first three years of Parrish's deanship, Maurer saw the addition of highly qualified scholars, including Gina-Gail Fletcher, Pamela Foohey, Jessica Eaglin, and David Gamage, as well as Clinical Professor Norm Hedges and Professor of Practice Shana Wallace. Honors and new opportunities for fellow faculty members included Professor Jeanine Bell's appointment as editor of the prestigious *Law and Society Review.* Professor Bill Henderson was named the most influential

Since 1975, Baier has been active in the Boone and Crockett Club, America's oldest wildlife conservation organization founded by Theodore Roosevelt in 1887, and is its first president emeritus. A well-known advisor to elected officials and educators on environmental and conservation issues, he took the lead in drafting President George H. W. Bush's wildlife conservation agenda in 1989 and has been an advisor and counselor to all successive presidential administrations. From 1992 until 2010, Baier led in the creation of PhD programs dedicated to postgraduate studies in natural resources and wildlife conservation management at five universities. Between 2004 and 2007, he led a national campaign to raise $6.5 million for the federal government to purchase the last and largest piece of privately held original land remaining from Theodore Roosevelt's historic Elkhorn Ranch, established in 1884 adjacent to the Theodore Roosevelt National Park. Baier is also the author of the book *Inside the Equal Access to Justice Act: Environmental Litigation and the Crippling Battle over America's Lands, Endangered Species, and Their Critical Habitat*, published in 2015.

He has served on numerous boards and commissions for both local and federal governments, associations, and foundations. Among those are the Executive Committee of the Theodore Roosevelt Association, President's Council of the National Wildlife Federation, the National Conservation Leadership Institute where he is vice chairman, the Conservation Leadership Council sponsored by the Environmental Defense Fund, and the Roosevelt-Rockefeller Brothers Conservation Roundtable.

He has been recognized many times for his public service and conservation work. In 2010, *Outdoor Life* magazine selected Baier as the Conservationist of the Year, and the Association of Fish and Wildlife Agencies similarly recognized him in 2013. In 2016, the National Wildlife Federation awarded him their highest honor: the Jay N. "Ding" Darling Conservation Award for a lifetime of conservation service. The Maurer School of Law presented him with its Distinguished Service Award in 2007, and in 2014, he was inducted into the Academy of Law Alumni Fellows. In recognition of his generous gift to the Maurer School of Law, the law building was named Baier Hall in 2015.

person in legal education by the *National Jurist* in both 2015 and 2016, and Professors Victor Quintanilla and Jody Madeira were named as codirectors of the Center for Law, Society, and Culture. In 2017, the Bradley Fellows in Criminal Law and Procedure was also founded as part of the Center for Law, Society, and Culture. Named in honor of the late Professor Craig Bradley, the Bradley Fellows was created to prepare Maurer law students for successful careers in criminal justice as prosecutors, public defenders, private criminal defense attorneys, and policy makers. Joe Hoffmann, the Harry Pratter Professor of Law, serves as the

# ENDOWED CHAIRS AND PROFESSORSHIPS

The law school has established endowed chairs and professorships to provide recognition and support to law faculty for outstanding scholarship. The first named professorship, the Walter W. Foskett Professorship, was awarded to William Popkin in 1987 for his nationally recognized scholarship in tax, legislation, and statutory interpretation. During Fred Aman's deanship, the number of named professorships increased from two to fourteen. Thanks to the continued generosity of donors, today there are more than twenty chairs and professorships available to law faculty.

One of the faculty currently holding endowed professorships is David Fidler, the James L. Calamaras Professor of Law. Fidler specializes in international law, national security, and emerging technologies. He is a leading expert on cybersecurity law and policy and is also an internationally recognized expert on global health and biosecurity threats. Robert Fischman, the George P. Smith II Distinguished Professor of Law, is a leading expert on the relationship between law and conservation implementation and is a coauthor of the leading casebook on public land and resources law. Donna Nagy, the C. Ben Dutton Professor of Law, is a nationally recognized expert on securities litigation, securities regulations, and corporations and has coauthored two books and numerous articles. The John F. Kimberling Professor of Law is held by Charles Geyh, whose expertise is in the areas of judicial conduct, ethics, procedure, independence, accountability, and administration. Geyh has authored numerous books and articles and was named an Andrew Carnegie Fellow in 2016.

Dawn Johnsen, the current Walter W. Foskett Professor of Law, came to the law school following a distinguished career in Washington, DC. Her research centers on issues of separation of powers (especially presidential power) and civil liberties (especially reproductive rights). Kevin Brown is the Richard S. Melvin Professor of Law. Brown's scholarship focuses on the areas of race, law, and education, and he has written numerous books and articles on the subject. William Henderson, the Stephen F. Burns Professor of Law, has devoted much of his scholarship to empirical analysis of the legal profession and legal education. He is considered one of the country's leading experts on trends in the legal profession. The John E. Schiller Chair in Legal Ethics is held by Hannah Buxbaum, whose research is in the areas of private international law and international litigation and jurisdiction. She publishes widely in both US and European journals and is the coauthor of a leading casebook on international business transactions.

Law faculty also hold university professorships. In addition to being named the C. Ben Dutton Professor of Law, Fred Cate was awarded the rank of distinguished professor by the university in 2003. One of the foremost authorities in information privacy and security law issues, Cate has authored more than 150 articles and books and was the founding director of the university's Center for Applied Cybersecurity Research, where he is now a senior fellow. In 2018, Christiana Ochoa was named a Class of 1950 Herman B Wells Endowed Professor. Ochoa has worked extensively in Latin America, and her scholarship has focused on governance in the field of business and human rights.

**FIG. 4.21.** Law School faculty, 2016–17. Photographer: Deborah W. Conkle. *Jerome Hall Law Library Archives 029\2016.FACG.1.*

director. He is a nationally recognized authority on the death penalty and has also written extensively on criminal procedure and habeas corpus law.

In February 2017, Dean Parrish announced a partnership with the Southern Poverty Law Center for a scholarship, mentoring, and summer-externship program designed to attract high-performing law students interested in social justice and equity issues. In August 2017, Maurer and the IU Wells Scholars program announced a plan that would allow Wells Scholars to earn both a bachelor's degree and a JD in six years instead of seven. These and other programs would complement an expanding array of new master's and PhD programs, including a master's in cybersecurity and a doctorate of philosophy in law and democracy. The close of 2017 saw the successful conclusion of another ABA-AALS reaccreditation inspection, the 25th anniversary of the *Indiana Journal of Global Legal Studies*, still headed by former Dean Fred Aman, and most remarkably, the School of Law's 175th anniversary.

No words can briefly or eloquently summarize the remarkable journey of the Indiana University Maurer School of Law, from its humble beginnings as the law department under David McDonald and his handful of students in December of 1842 to the law school of the early twenty-first century, with over sixty active and prolific faculty members, over 720 current students, and more than ten thousand alumni around the globe, many of whom continue to be involved in many important ways. Every single person who has ever been involved with the Maurer Law community should take great pride in the enormous strides the school has taken and, as Colleen Pauwels wrote twenty-five years ago, "of the dreams realized and the challenges well met" (Pauwels 1992, 36). And to those who will come to Maurer Law after us, we should also say thank-you for continuing the pursuit of excellence and for all of your efforts to ensure that Maurer Law remains a school "inferior to none."

FIG. 5.1. Jerome Hall Law Library, looking into reading room from outside. *Jerome Hall Law Library Archives*.

# 5 | JEROME HALL LAW LIBRARY

A $100 ALLOCATION FROM THE BOARD OF trustees for the purchase of law books in 1843 marked the beginning of the law library collection. Although belonging to the university library, law books were selected by Professor McDonald and housed in his office. The first real mention of the law library was in the university *Catalogue* for 1847, which noted that there was a "good law library" but gave no real information. Tragically, this collection was consumed by the fire of April 1854 that destroyed the First College Building. A brick building was erected after the fire, and the law library was housed in a room separate from the university library. This arrangement was made to give law students more access to the collection, as the university library was only open on Saturday mornings.

**FIG. 5.2.** Law library in Kirkwood Hall. This image appeared on page 28 of the booklet *Indiana University, Bloomington*, published in March 1900. The date of the photo is unknown, but the law library resided in Kirkwood Hall from 1895–1901. *IU Archives P0022241.*

In the early 1870s, law classes were held in a space downtown due to overcrowded conditions on campus. Only a portion of the law library was moved to this location, which did not make the law students happy. There is no mention as to whether the students were successful in having the entire collection moved, but the problem was rectified after law classes were moved back to campus in 1874. When the law department was suspended in 1877, the collection remained with the university library. During this time, disaster struck once again when the university library was consumed by fire in 1883.

When the School of Law reopened in 1889, a new law library, with a collection of about 2,500 volumes, was established soon after. The new library, located with the Law School, contained a full selection of textbooks and case reports; the collection was placed with the law school so that law students and faculty could have easy access to the specialized materials. From this time forward, the law library has always been in the same building as the law school.

Having outgrown its space in Maxwell Hall, the law school moved to Kirkwood Hall in 1895 and moved once again, in 1901, to Wylie Hall. By this time

FIG. 5.3. Students studying in the law library, Wylie Hall. Circa 1901. *Jerome Hall Law Library Archives 010\2014.HIST.13.*

the library's collection had grown to about 4,500 volumes, including the entire national reporter system, federal reporters, official state reports, and the leading law journals. Hours were increased to allow more time for law student access, offering uninterrupted hours from 7:40 a.m. to 9:50 p.m. Prior to this, the library was closed several times a day during recitation and chapel hours. The law library was a popular place for students to study and conduct research. The student newspaper reported that the best testimonial to the library's popularity was that the janitor could find no time between 7:00 a.m. and 10:00 p.m. in which to clean the library. He was quoted as saying, "There's too many fellows live here. I guess they ain't got nowhere else to stay" (*Daily Student*, December 19, 1905, 1).

When the law school returned to Maxwell Hall in 1908, the university lacked the funds to move the law library in one day. Not wanting to be without a library for even a few days, law students volunteered to move the books themselves. Under Dean Hogate's supervision, seventy-five law students moved the six thousand volumes on a Saturday morning in just two hours! Floyd Newsom (LLB; 1908) was in charge of preparing the books, and Frank Wade (LLB; 1908) carried the first box to Maxwell Hall. Clifton Williams (LLB; 1908) supervised the arrangement of the

**FIG. 5.4.** Samuel S. Dargan standing on front steps of Maxwell Hall. Circa 1919. Dargan served as curator of the law library for many years. Photographer: Charles Gilbert Shaw. *IU Archives P0020869.*

books on the shelves. The *Daily Student*, reporting on the move, quoted Dean Hogate as saying, "This action, voluntary as it was, illustrates the interest our law students have in the school. They wanted to get in the commodious new building quickly; and they were willing to sacrifice energy to get there" ("School of Law in Its New Home," *Daily Student*, February 10, 1908, 1). With this move, the law library occupied four rooms on the first floor of Maxwell Hall.

Funding the law library was one of the school's biggest problems. President Bryan brought the need for additional money to the attention of the board of trustees in November 1908, when he asked for $2,000 for the law library. The trustees did not agree to that amount but did allocate $1,000 for the library. Dean Hogate asked for a special appropriation for the library in 1912, this time receiving a $1,300 allocation. The library's collection jumped substantially between 1914 and 1915, from seven thousand to twelve thousand volumes. However, this growth cannot be entirely attributed to additional funding; as three thousand volumes were found for which there had been no records.

Until 1908, the law library was managed entirely by a law student chosen each year by the dean. It did not always run smoothly; the student newspaper reported complaints from time to time, mostly about missing books and slow reshelving of books.

In 1908, Sam Dargan, class of 1909 and the first African American graduate of the school, was hired as curator of the law library, at a salary of $300 per year; in addition to this, he ran the student bookstore. Until 1921, one student assistant was also hired to manage the library. After that time, as the library grew larger, two or more students worked as assistants. Among the familiar names who helped run the library during this time were Ross Franklin Lockridge in 1906 (father of Ross Lockridge Jr., author of *Raintree County*), Sherman Minton in 1915, and Walter Treanor in 1922 (Lowell 1957, 423).

By 1925, the law library had grown to the point that an experienced librarian was needed to catalog and maintain the collection. Rowena Compton was hired as the first librarian for the

FIG. 5.5. Rowena Compton served as the first law librarian from 1925 until 1930. Date and origin of photo unknown. *Jerome Hall Law Library Archives.*

law library in September 1925. Highly qualified, she held an LLB from Washington College of Law and had previous library experience at the Orleans Public Library in Indiana, the Department of the Interior, and the Library of Congress. Shortly after her arrival, the law library was established as a separate collection from the university library. Although physically separate for many years, the university library had been responsible for ordering and cataloging books for the law library. Unfortunately, illness forced Compton to resign from her position in October 1930, and she died shortly after in Orleans, Indiana.

Mary Jean Ashman succeeded Compton in February 1931. Ashman earned an AB from Indiana University in 1927. Prior to her arrival, she had been a librarian at the State University of Iowa. While serving as law librarian, she began taking classes at the law school, finally completing her LLB in 1962. In addition to her responsibilities in the library, Ashman was editor of the *Law Library Journal* from November 1942 to May 1946, and she assumed the title of instructor, legal bibliography at the law school beginning in September 1946.

At the time of Ashman's arrival, the law library had grown to more than twenty thousand volumes. Finances were still tight, but a number of important

## FIRST LEGAL RESEARCH COURSE

In November 1923, Dean Hepburn announced a new course on how to use the books in the law library. According to the *Indiana Daily Student* on November 27, 1923, he stated that the purpose of the course was to enable students to use the books in *any* law library. A year later Hepburn announced that a library seminar had been organized for freshman law students and that they would be personally instructed in how to use the law library. Students would be taught how to find cases and statutes, how to run down later authorities after a case has been found, and how to understand the abbreviations used by reporters and courts. On November 18, 1924, the student newspaper reported that William O. Wilson and Jesse W. McAtee, senior law students, would be the first instructors.

**FIG. 5.6.** Jean Ashman (*right*), law librarian from 1931 to 1949, with her assistant, Elsie Langohr. 1940. Photographer: Everett E. Mitchell. *Jerome Hall Law Library Archives 010\2014.HIST.15.*

FIG. 5.7. Law library reading room, Maxwell Hall. 1940. *IU Archives P0027473.*

donations improved the depth of the collection. In 1931, Addison L. Roache, a member of the board of trustees and a justice of the Indiana Supreme Court, gave the library a collection of early session laws of Indiana from his private collection, which completed the library's holdings of Indiana session laws. Substantial donations also came from law firms and even from the St. Meinrad Abbey. During Paul McNutt's tenure as governor from 1933–37, the legislature passed laws giving the law school sufficient copies of the state session laws and other state reports for both the library's collection and for exchanges with other libraries, which enabled the library to build its state collection at minimal cost. Additionally, copies of the

**FIG. 5.8.** Students working diligently in a corner of the law library, Maxwell Hall. 1941.
*IU Archives P0038060.*

## BETTY VIRGINIA LEBUS

Betty V. LeBus was born in Bremerton, Washington, on May 8, 1923. She attended the University of Washington in Seattle, receiving a BS in 1947, LLB in 1948, and BA in library science in 1949, one of the first graduates of the prestigious law librarian program at the University of Washington. LeBus came to Indiana in 1950 when she accepted an offer to be law librarian, a position she held for twenty-eight years. At the time of her arrival, LeBus was the only woman on the law faculty. In 1957, she was granted tenure, becoming the first woman to receive tenure at the law school, and in 1977, she was promoted to full professor of law.

LeBus held many leadership roles in law and library organizations. She was active in the American Association of Law Libraries, serving on many committees as well as the executive board. She was a law school site evaluator for the American Bar Association for many years, and she also served as president of the Indiana Library Association in 1961. In 1964, the Indiana Library Trustee Association named her librarian of the year.

Betty LeBus resigned in 1978 to return to Seattle to be with her elderly mother. But her career as a law librarian was not over. She eventually returned to work, first as law librarian at the University of Wyoming and then completing her career at the University of Miami. LeBus returned to Bloomington following her retirement in 1984, where she passed away on August 24, 2003.

FIG. SIDEBAR 5.2. Betty V. LeBus, director of the law library, 1950–78. 1960. *Jerome Hall Law Library Archives* 010\2014.HIST.6.

**FIG. 5.9.** Library reading room in the newly constructed law building. Circa 1956. *Jerome Hall Law Library Archives img480.*

*Indiana Law Journal* were exchanged with other law school libraries, further strengthening the collection at little or no cost.

In late 1936, the university's administrative offices moved to the newly constructed administration building, Bryan Hall, giving the law school the entirety of Maxwell Hall and expanding space for the law library. The reading room was greatly enlarged, and study tables and chairs were added, nearly doubling the seating capacity. Three large rooms in the basement were added to hold parts of the growing collection.

Ashman resigned as law librarian in 1949 to accept a position at the University of Chicago, and Betty V. LeBus was appointed to succeed Ashman in 1950. Prior to her appointment, LeBus had served for a short time as an assistant librarian at the University of Washington in Seattle. At IU, she held the position of law librarian

**FIG. 5.10.** Students researching and studying in the law library. Circa 1956. *Jerome Hall Law Library Archives img481.*

and instructor of law. The only woman on the law faculty at the time, she taught legal research methods to all law students.

By this time, the collection had grown to fifty-seven thousand volumes, and the library, as well as the entire law school, was running out of space in Maxwell Hall. Shortly after LeBus arrived, planning began for the construction of a new building, the first to be built specifically for the law school. LeBus was instrumental in this process and served as the law school's project manager during the planning and construction phases, completed in 1956.

Faced with moving the entire library collection to another building, the school once again turned to law students. With LeBus coordinating the effort, student volunteers moved approximately seventy-five thousand books through the woods from Maxwell Hall to the new law building, a much bigger move than in 1908!

Among student volunteers were Leroy W. Hofmann, Robert Ruddell, Lester A. Kassing, Philip C. Potts, Frank A. Webster, Gene E. Brooks, and Frank Barnhart. By all accounts, the move went very smoothly.

The new library had seating for 235 persons and space for approximately 130,000 volumes (LeBus 1957, 214). A traditional high-ceiling reading room had been considered but was rejected in favor of an open space, integrating study space with stack areas. It was thought that this would give more flexibility for future years. Individual study carrels and group tables were distributed throughout the library, and there was an office for the law librarian and a large room for the staff. It was luxurious at the time, but within two decades the library would once again be facing a serious space problem.

Even with a new building, the law school was faced with substantial financial problems in the latter 1950s and 1960s. The growth of the law library slowed, and by the mid-1960s, its holdings numbered approximately one hundred thousand volumes. The depth of the library's research collection was greatly enhanced in 1964 when it acquired one of the largest collections of US Supreme Court Records and Briefs in existence from the Indiana Supreme Court. This three-thousand-volume acquisition, dating back to 1925, was negotiated by President Elvis Stahr and Professor Howard Mann. Additionally, an agreement was reached with the US Supreme Court to add the law library to the list a depository libraries for all future briefs of the court. At that time, thirty public and educational libraries served as depositories for the briefs in print. Today, the law library still serves as a depository, now one of only ten remaining libraries to serve in that capacity.

By the mid-1960s, the library was feeling squeezed from the effects of an increased student enrollment and the growth of the collection. This was temporarily alleviated when the law school recovered the ground floor of the law building, which had been used by the Indiana State Geological Survey. The library received a substantial amount of this space and was able to add seating as well as shelving.

The 1960s was a time of great expansion of the law into new areas, and its already inadequate budget made it difficult for the library to build new relevant collections. By 1968, Dean Burnett Harvey saw the law library as the most immediate problem to be addressed, both in terms of space and budget. In a February 1968 interview in the law school publication, *I-Witness*, he speculated that the library would be out of shelf space in five years at its current rate of growth. He also expressed concern about the book budget, which at that time was determined in conjunction with the university library's budget. He wished to bring the law library's total budget within the school so that the development of the library could be planned in conjunction with other areas of the school. The library's budget was

## COLLEEN KRISTL PAUWELS

Colleen K. Pauwels was born in Chicago, Illinois, on January 26, 1946, and grew up in South Bend, Indiana. She received a BA from Barat College in 1968 and her MLS in 1975 and JD in 1986 both from Indiana University. She accepted an appointment as public services librarian at the law library shortly after completing her MLS. She was named interim director in 1978, which was assumed to be a temporary appointment. However, Pauwels was a natural fit for the position, and she became the permanent director and associate professor of law in 1983. In her thirty-three years as director, she transformed the library from a facility that struggled to meet the basic needs of its patrons to a nationally recognized research library.

Pauwels was an integral part of the planning and construction of the library addition and renovation, completed in 1986. Following this, she was actively involved in every construction project at the law school until her retirement in 2011. An interest in history led her to become the unofficial historian of the law school, and she published numerous articles relating to its history. At the time of her retirement in 2011, she was the longest-serving director in the law library's history. In recognition of her service, she was inducted into the Academy of Law Alumni Fellows in 2013. She died on April 24, 2013, at the age of sixty-seven.

FIG. SIDEBAR 5.3. Colleen K. Pauwels, director of the law library, 1978–2011. Photo taken in 2011 on the occasion of her retirement. Photographer: Tom Casalini. *Jerome Hall Law Library Archives 001\2013. ALAF.116.*

moved under the law school, but it would be years before the financial and space issues were successfully addressed.

The library's problems only grew in the 1970s. As predicted, it was out of space and lacked adequate seating for its growing student body. The problem became so severe that the ABA-AALS inspection team in the mid-1970s cited the conditions

**FIG. 5.11.** Atrium and reading room in Jerome Hall Law Library. 2014. Photographer: Zach Hetrick. *Maurer School of Law Photo Archive.*

in the library as a serious defect. The seating problem was temporarily alleviated by repurposing a lounge into a study room with additional seating for students, but other space issues could not be solved within the existing building.

Even with these challenges, the School of Law library was making progress in other areas. Although the staff was still small compared to other law libraries, it was increased in response to the need to provide more services to the growing faculty and student body. By 1976, there were five librarians including Betty LeBus, as well as four full-time support staff. The library had joined OCLC, a cooperative network of libraries, to catalog its books. In 1977, the library was an early subscriber to Lexis, bringing online legal research capabilities to law students and faculty for the first time, and a subscription to Westlaw followed in 1983. It would be many years before these systems replaced any part of the print collection, but the digital revolution had begun.

In 1978, after twenty-eight years at the school, Betty LeBus resigned suddenly to return to Seattle and assist her elderly mother. Colleen K. Pauwels, public services librarian at the time, assumed the role of acting director. After serving in an interim capacity for five years, she was appointed director of the law library and associate professor of law in 1983.

FIG. 5.12. Students conversing and relaxing in the lobby of the law library. Since opening in 1986, the lobby has been the most popular student gathering place between classes. *Jerome Hall Law Library Archives.*

The fortunes of the law library began to improve after Sheldon J. Plager was appointed dean in 1977 and received a commitment from the university administration to provide substantial increases to the library's acquisitions budget, to increase its staff, and to support a building addition. At the time of his arrival, the library had the smallest acquisitions budget of all the Big Ten law libraries. The university committed to increasing the allocation until it was at the median of these budgets.

The university followed through on its promises, making the 1980s a time of unprecedented growth and change for the law library. When Plager arrived, the acquisitions budget was $115,000. By 1980, it had grown to $212,000, and by 1990, it was $933,000. The library was able not only to expand its holdings into emerging areas of law but also to purchase important retrospective collections, beyond the capacity of the budget in previous years. The law library was finally evolving into a major research library.

Solving the space issues took time, but in 1981, an addition to the building was approved, primarily for the law library. Pauwels was instrumental in planning and overseeing the construction of the new space. Upon completion of the addition,

**FIG. 5.13.** Since 1989, the law library has hosted the annual party for graduating students and their families the evening before commencement. 2017. Photographer: Deborah W. Conkle. *Jerome Hall Law Library 035\2018.EVENT.7–41.*

the existing building was renovated, and the entire project was finished in 1986. This time the collection was too large to be moved by volunteer law students, and a professional company was hired to complete the move over semester break.

The library addition, located on six levels, more than doubled its shelving capacity. It also included small group-study rooms and ample seating. The staff work areas were spacious, with room for growth. Moreover, it was a beautiful space, with an open atrium and floor-to-ceiling windows overlooking Dunn's Woods. The expansive lobby at the entrance to the library, separate from the study areas, quickly became a gathering space for students between classes.

By the 1990s, the IU School of Law's library was firmly established as one of the finest law libraries in the country. The staff had nearly tripled in size from the 1970s, with a number of law-trained reference librarians available to assist faculty and students. In 1990, the collection included over three hundred thousand bound

How your dog can help you find a law job **24**

Are law students in danger from terrorists? **14**

Bio-terrorism, Genetics: LL.M.s for the 21st centruy **35**

# the National Jurist

THE MAGAZINE FOR LAW STUDENTS          OCTOBER 2004 VOL. 14, NO. 2

Why Indiana Outranks Harvard

BEST LAW LIBRARIES

**PLUS**

**Montana** in fight with conservative prof, **Detroit Mercy** runs clinic from RV, **Duke** changes grading policy, **Florida A&M, Florida International** get ABA accreditation, **Berkeley** students protest Iraq war

FIG. 5.14. Indiana University Law Library tied with the University of Iowa as the "best law library in the country," according to *National Jurist* magazine in 2004. *Cover credit: Cypress Magazines.*

**FIG. 5.15.** Linda K. Fariss, director of the law library, 2011–16. Photo taken in 2016 on the occasion of her retirement. Photographer: Tom Casalini. *Jerome Hall Law Library Archives 030\2016. FAC.1.*

volumes and nearly one million microform pieces. The first online catalog was functional by 1990, and plans were well underway for other online modules, such as an automated circulation system. Print collections were continuing to grow, not yet replaced with electronic resources, but both Lexis and Westlaw were now available on individual desktops, replacing dedicated computers.

By 2000, the digital revolution was in full swing. Libraries were beginning to cancel print subscriptions in favor of a digital format, and the law library was no exception. As the acquisitions budget, now $1.3 million, flatlined and space once again became an issue, the library canceled and discarded some print materials. Fortunately, the university libraries now had a state-of-the-art storage facility, allowing the library to place seldom-used-but-valuable print collections in retrievable storage.

## JEROME HALL LAW LIBRARY

In 2015, the law library was named for Jerome
Hall, a former distinguished member of the law
school faculty. The naming was made possible
by a generous gift from alumnus Lowell E. Baier,
class of 1964, who requested that the library be
named for Jerome Hall, his professor and mentor.
Hall was a member of the faculty from 1939 until
his retirement in 1970. A beloved teacher and
prolific scholar, he was known worldwide for his
scholarship in criminal law and jurisprudence
and was a pioneer in the interdisciplinary analysis
of legal issues, an area in which the law school
continues to excel.

At the naming ceremony on May 8, 2015,
Lowell Baier stated, "I am deeply honored by the
opportunity to make this gift to the Law School.
In particular, I am pleased that the library will
be renamed in honor of Professor Hall, whose
teaching and mentoring were so crucial to my
success as a student, and whose wisdom has
continued to guide me throughout my career. This
gift will ensure the continuing integrity of the
law school building and the law library, its very
soul, inspiring the best in academic and scholastic
achievement—remember, a sense of place creates
a sense of purpose" ("Baier Hall and Jerome Hall
Law Library Naming Ceremony," May 8, 2015,
https://www.repository.law.indiana.edu/mle/3/).

FIG. SIDEBAR 5.4. Lowell E. Baier at the entrance to
the Jerome Hall Law Library on the day of the naming
ceremony for the library and law building. May 8,
2015. Photographer: Deborah W. Conkle. *Jerome Hall
Law Library Archives 031\2017.EVENTS.6–56.*

After thirty-three years of directorship, Pauwels retired in 2011, having provided leadership for the most expansive period in the history of the law library.
Linda K. Fariss, the longtime associate director, was appointed director in an
interim capacity and became the permanent director of the law library and senior
lecturer in law in February 2012. Fariss received a BS degree in 1973, master of
library science (MLS) in 1980, and JD in 1988, all from Indiana University.

With the increased presence of electronic resources and the decline of print, a
law library was no longer measured solely on the size of its collection but also on

**FIG. 5.16.** Keith Buckley, director of the law library since 2017. 2013. Photographer: Ann Schertz. *Maurer School of Law Photo Archive.*

the services provided. During Fariss's tenure as director, the library focused on providing new services and looking at ways to improve services already in place. A new emphasis was placed on teaching, and the Advanced Legal Research course was offered to law students for the first time. The library had been serving as the print archive for many years and also had a diverse collection of personal papers, the largest being the papers of Wilbur Pell, who served as a judge for the US Court of Appeals for the Seventh Circuit from 1970 until 1984.

In late 2012, the library expanded its archival role by launching a digital repository, whose initial focus was to provide open access to faculty scholarship and later expanded to showcase the history of the law school. In 2015, Fariss signed an agreement with Judge David Hamilton of the US Court of Appeals for the Seventh Circuit, whose chambers are located in the law school, for the library to serve as the repository for his personal case files. The highlight of her tenure was the naming of the law library for Jerome Hall in 2015, made possible by a generous donation from alumnus Lowell Baier.

After serving the law library for over forty years, including nearly six as director, Fariss retired in early 2017. Keith Buckley, another longtime law librarian, was appointed interim director and became the permanent director of the law library and senior lecturer in law in December 2017. Buckley received his BS in 1977, MLS in 1980, and JD in 1989, all from Indiana University. With his background and experience, he is well suited to move the library forward and meet the challenges of a twenty-first-century library.

The Jerome Hall Law Library's history is nearly as long as the law school itself. From the beginning, it has been a central gathering place for law students. Although it has struggled at times due to space constraints and budget, it has remained an essential part of the law school. As Lowell Baier stated on May 8, 2015, in the library's naming ceremony, "This gift will ensure the continuing integrity of the law school building and the law library, its very soul, inspiring the best in academic and scholastic achievement—remember, a sense of place creates a sense of purpose."

## THE OWL AND THE SQUIRREL—
## ANIMALS IN THE LAW LIBRARY!

It's not unusual to find the occasional mouse, bird, or even bat in the law library. However, owls and squirrels are not everyday occurrences! On May 21, 1919, the *Indiana Daily Student* reported that an owl had been spotted perched on the window of the law library. According to the story, a crowd gathered to watch the owl, and eventually the students captured it under a wastepaper basket. The owl was adopted by the senior class in hopes that its wisdom would follow the class throughout life. No follow-up could be found on what happened to the owl, or if the story was even true.

The story of the squirrel is definitely true, as the authors witnessed it. On April 2, 1991, a squirrel was spotted in the reference collection. Over a two-hour period, the chase was on, with students, library staff, and university pest-control personnel in on the action. For most of that time, the squirrel was in control, effectively avoiding all attempts at capture. Pandemonium ensued in the library as students gathered around the atrium on all floors to view the chase and cheer on the squirrel! Finally, Jack Past, then a second-year law student, captured the squirrel by throwing a coat over it and picking it up. The squirrel had one last attempt at freedom when it bit Jack's finger, but Jack held on (and fortunately he was fine). Bloomington Animal Control took custody of the squirrel, and it was released after being kept for observation. Just another day at the law library!

FIG. 6.1. Group of international students celebrating graduation. Photographer: Randy Johnson. *Jerome Hall Law Library Archives 009.2013.LAWPUBS.2–4.*

# 6 | INTERNATIONAL STUDENTS AND THE RISE OF GRADUATE LEGAL STUDIES PROGRAMS

INDIANA UNIVERSITY OPENED ITS DOORS TO international students early in the twentieth century, and the law school was among the first departments to welcome these students. Four young men from the Philippines arrived at Indiana University in 1904 as part of a federal program, referred to as the Pensionado Program, that brought top Filipino students to the United States to study at select universities. These four were the first of numerous Filipinos to attend IU through this program.

FIG. 6.2. Jorge Bocobo, along with Francisco Delgado and Mariano H. de Joya, the first international students to attend the law school, receiving LLBs in 1907. *IU Archives P0079319.*

Three of these students, Francisco A. Delgado, Jorge C. Bocobo, and Mariano H. de Joya, enrolled in the law school in 1904 and graduated with an LLB in 1907. On completion of their education, the Pensionado students were required to return to the Philippines for a period of government service before embarking on their ultimate careers. All three excelled academically and became leaders in their country. Delgado became Philippine ambassador to the United States and the United Nations; Bocobo became a professor of law at the University of the Philippines School of Law, later dean of the law school and president of the university; and de Joya, who had a very successful private practice, also became a professor of law at the University of the Philippines and a member of the Philippine cabinet. Both Bocobo and Delgado received honorary degrees from Indiana University. Three wings of McNutt Dormitory on the IU Bloomington campus are named for these distinguished graduates.

The Filipino students immersed themselves in university life, participating in student organizations and social functions on campus. However, life in the United States was not always easy for them as some people in Indiana questioned their presence at the university and their mingling with the other students. Some citizens felt so strongly that a resolution was introduced in the legislature in 1909 to prevent a white woman from marrying a man with more than one-eighth Filipino blood. The student newspaper felt too much was made of this issue and offered assurance that the student body was supportive of the students. On receiving word of these issues, a representative from the Bureau of Insular Affairs came to Bloomington to investigate whether the Filipino students were being treated fairly

# FRANCISCO A. DELGADO

Francisco A. Delgado was born in Bulacan Province, Philippine Islands, in 1886. He arrived in Bloomington with three other Filipino students in 1904. After receiving his LLB in 1907, Delgado was admitted to the bar of Indiana. The following year he attended Yale University, receiving an LLM in 1908. Upon his return to the Philippines in 1908, he worked for the government, fulfilling his required government service. Following that, he began private practice in Manila, quickly becoming a distinguished trial lawyer. In 1919, Delgado was the first Filipino to become an active member of the American Bar Association.

Delgado served as a representative in the Philippine legislature from 1931 to 1934. A believer in rights for all, he fought for the passage of a bill to grant Filipino women the right to appear in court and transact business without their husbands. He returned to the United States in 1934 to become resident commissioner from the Philippines to the US Congress, a position he held until 1936, when he returned to Manila to serve as a justice for the Court of Appeals.

During the Japanese invasion of Manila in World War II, Delgado was captured and tortured, likely due to his association with the United States. He eventually escaped, living in a cave with his wife until the island was liberated by US forces ("Top Dividends from Investment," *Indiana Alumni Magazine*, May 1961, 25). Following the war, he returned to the United States as a delegate of the Philippines to the International Committee of Jurists and was also a delegate to the United Nations Conference in San Francisco, signing the UN Charter for the Philippines. From 1946 to 1951, he served as the commissioner of the Philippine War Damage Commission, the only non–American citizen to hold a presidential appointment confirmed by the US Senate. He was elected to the Philippine senate in 1951, serving until 1957.

In 1958, Delgado returned to the United Nations upon his appointment as ambassador extraordinary and plenipotentiary and permanent Philippine delegate, where he served until his retirement in 1962. While delivering a fiery anti-communist speech, he became the subject of one of Khrushchev's famous "table poundings." During his time there, Delgado was one of the most respected and admired delegates. In 1945, he received an honorary degree from Indiana University, the place he considered his second home. The citation read, "Francisco Afan Delgado, your life and deed exemplify the concept of world brotherhood which provides the only lasting basis for peace. Patriot, soldier, uncompromising resistance leader during the Japanese occupation of your homeland, teacher, jurist, statesman, world citizen, your Alma Mater gladly confers upon you the degree Doctor of Laws" ("Top Dividends from Investment," 25). Delgado died in Manila in 1964.

FIG. SIDEBAR 6.1. Francisco A. Delgado. 1907. *IU Archives P0022342.*

## MASUJI MIYAKAWA

Masuji Miyakawa, born in 1870 in Fukushima, Japan, came to the United States in 1896, settling in San Francisco. After working a variety of jobs, including proprietor and editor of the *Japan Tribune* newspaper, Miyakawa traveled east to attend George Washington University (at the time called Columbian College), where he received an LLM in 1903. He then came to Indiana University in 1904, earning his LLB in 1905 and also receiving a doctor of civil law (DCL) from Illinois College of Law (now DePaul University School of Law) in the same year. While at Indiana, he became a naturalized US citizen. Miyakawa was admitted to the bar, becoming the first Japanese American admitted to practice in the United States.

Miyakawa practiced law and served as an advocate for the rights of Japanese immigrants. In 1906, he was chief counsel for the schoolchildren in a landmark civil rights case in which the San Francisco school board, responding to anti-Japanese sentiment, forced Japanese children in the city to attend segregated schools. Miyakawa and the Japanese community mobilized opinion in both the Unites States and Japan, and before the case was decided, the federal government intervened. President Theodore Roosevelt asked the school board to revoke their policy, and, in exchange, he would restrict Japanese laborers from entering the country. They agreed, and Roosevelt brokered a resolution with the Japanese government known as the Gentleman's Agreement, where Japan agreed not to grant exit visas to laborers in exchange for assurance that immigrants could still bring their families to the United States. Even though the case was never decided, Miyakawa's defense of the Japanese made him famous nationally.

Miyakawa was a prolific writer and lecturer. He worked with the American Bar Association in its early years, serving as editor for Japan of the *Bulletin of the Comparative Law Bureau*. The author of books on both Japanese life and culture as well as American law, among his publications are *Life of Japan* (1907) and *Powers of the American People, Congress, President, and Courts: According to the Evolution of the Constitutional Construction* (1908). He made several tours lecturing about Japan and also founded *Japan Review* magazine in 1913.

While on a mission for the Japanese consul following the outbreak of World War I in 1914, Miyakawa became very ill. He never fully recovered and died in 1916 (Robinson 2016, 157). He was inducted into the Academy of Law Alumni Fellows in 2006.

FIG. SIDEBAR 6.2. Masuji Miyakawa, 1905. *Jerome Hall Law Library Archives 001\2013.ALAF.117.*

but agreed with the newspaper that the issue was without merit and decided to let the students remain, primarily due to their academic success (Clark 1973, 41–42).

The original Pensionado Program ended in 1914, but these students formed the beginning of a long relationship between the law school and the Philippines. Many Filipino students attended the school over the next fifty years, such as Juan T. Santos, who received an LLB in 1916, and Flerida Ruth P. Romero, who received an LLM in 1955. Santos became a judge and law professor, and Romero enjoyed a long and illustrious career, culminating in her appointment as associate justice of the Supreme Court of the Philippines in 1991. In fact, Santos wrote a letter recommending Romero for admission to the law school, demonstrating the importance of alumni connections, even in the early years (Romero 2012, 175).

At the same time the Filipino students were arriving on campus, the university also began receiving students from China and Japan. Masuji Miyakawa enrolled in the law school as a third-year student in 1904. Having previously lived in San Francisco and Washington, DC, he told the *Indiana Daily Student* in an interview on November 4, 1904, that he came to Indiana to refresh his memory on certain legal subjects and to learn new points as well as to practice his English away from other Japanese speakers. A popular speaker on campus, he became a naturalized citizen of the United States while at the university.

These early foreign students all came to the school to obtain an LLB, the only law degree offered at the time. The faculty expressed interest in offering graduate degrees as early as 1908, but it took several years for it to become a reality. The JD degree was first offered in 1917 (discussed in chap. 2), and the LLM was offered for the first time in 1918. Although not originally conceived as a degree for foreign students already holding a law degree from their country, the LLM became primarily awarded for that purpose. A number of requirements were established for the degree: the candidate must have earned an LLB or equivalent degree from Indiana University or another school approved by the law school faculty, one additional year in residence at the Law School was required, during that fourth year the student had to complete at least eight hours a week of new courses with a record of superior character, and a thesis had to be completed and approved by the faculty. The first LLM was awarded in 1918 to Felino Lorenzo Merced, a Filipino student who had earned his LLB from Indiana University the previous year. It would be another five years before the second LLM was awarded, and the program remained small until the latter part of the twentieth century.

Between 1935 and 1950, numerous Chinese students came to US law schools to obtain a JD. Approximately thirty Chinese law students, both men and women, graduated from the Indiana University School of Law with a JD during this period, one of the largest numbers of any US law school. Nearly all of these students came

**FIG. 6.3.** Group of Chinese students at IU in 1935. Among those in the photograph are law students Lloyd Chang (*back row, middle*), Tao Cheng (*back row, right*), Ya Hui Hsu (*front row, middle*), and Liang Sun (*front row, right*). *IU Archives P0031217.*

from Soochow Law School in Shanghai, where they had already earned an LLB. Because of this, they were able to graduate with a JD in only three semesters. It is unknown what brought them to Indiana University, but these early Chinese students called IU "Yin Zhou" university, which translates to "green grass state university" (Wei Wang, Fudan Law School, email to Linda Fariss, November 4, 2016). The last of these students graduated in 1951 when the program ended, likely due to the Cultural Revolution in China.

Little information is known about these graduates, but one, Tongkui Ju (JD; 1949), received the Thomas Hart Benton Medal from Indiana University in 2013. This honor is given to individuals who have achieved a level of distinction in public office or service and have exemplified the values of Indiana University. Ju served as a judge in Shanghai district court and worked on some of the largest joint-venture and private-direct investment activities in China. Unfortunately, at

FIG. 6.4. German lawyers in 1950 attending the US State Department program following World War II. *Left to right, row 1:* Walter F. Rauer, Woldemar Heideman, Franz Ulrich Simon, Friedrich Joutz. *Row 2:* Gerold Blumenstein, Professor Ritchie Davis (program director), Ernst Schneider. *Row 3:* Hans Jurgen Dettmers, Professor Harry Pratter (instructor); Otto Carl Carllson, Hellmut von Stockhausen. *IU Archives P0079338.*

least one graduate, and perhaps others, was imprisoned following the Cultural Revolution. The law school received word through a prospective student from China that a 1949 graduate, Ming Shan Lee, served a prison term of five years, likely in part due to his American education.

Bloomington became home to a significant group of East European and German immigrants who left Europe during and just after the war. President Herman Wells was committed to expanding the international scope of the university and had spent time in Germany following World War II as special advisor to General Lucius D. Clay, responsible for, among others things, rebuilding the German educational system, including higher education. Wells's time in Germany expanded his reputation and international network, possibly encouraging the influx of

**FIG. 6.5.** Professor Jost Delbrück (LLM; 1960), member of the faculty. Photo taken upon the occasion of his retirement in 2003. Photographer: Tom Casalini. *Jerome Hall Law Library Archives 001|2013.FAC.19.h.*

foreign students and faculty to Indiana University following the war. The law school benefitted from the arrival of an increased number of students from Germany as well as other European countries during this time.

The US Department of State engaged in an exchange program after the war where German citizens from various professions came to the United States to learn about life here. Indiana was one of three law schools in the country chosen to conduct a special training program for German legal specialists. Professor Ritchie Davis was selected to act as coordinator for the program. A group of nine men from Germany arrived for the fall semester of 1950 to complete the "reorientation" program, which centered on a seminar called American Institutions, developed and taught by Professor Harry Pratter in his first year at the law school. In addition to law school classes, the students attended courses in other departments of the university. Additional time was allotted for the men to spend time in the field observing the American legal system in action ("Programs for Germans . . ." *Indiana Alumni Magazine*, November 1950, 9).

The law school admitted several German students under a de facto exchange program with the University of Kiel. One student, Jost Delbrück, began his coursework in 1959, the third student to arrive at IU as part of the exchange program. Although homesick, Delbrück found Bloomington to be a congenial place for him in the postwar years. As he described it, "With all the destruction I'd seen in my younger years, to find a peaceful—but not boring—atmosphere was something quite impressive to me" ("Jost Delbrück at Home at IU" *Bill of Particulars*, Spring 2002, 30). He excelled at his studies, receiving an LLM in 1960, and while at the university, he developed a close, lifelong friendship with Professor Ralph Fuchs. Upon completion of his degree, he returned to Kiel to continue his education, becoming a world-renowned international-law scholar and teacher. Delbrück served

**FIG. 6.6.** Group photo of graduate students with Professor Gene Shreve. Summer 1996. Photographer: Randy Johnson. *Jerome Hall Law Library Archives 006\2013.STUD.21–32.*

as both the dean of the law school at the University of Kiel and as president and rector of the university. During this time, he maintained close ties with Indiana University, returning numerous times and encouraging promising German students to come to Bloomington. In 1990, Professor Delbrück joined the faculty of the law school, returning every fall to teach until his retirement in 2003.

Although foreign students had been an almost constant presence since the beginning of the twentieth century, no new programs had been developed outside of the small LLM program, until 1983, when the law school expanded the graduate studies program by adding an additional graduate degree, the master of comparative law (MCL). Also designed for foreign lawyers, this degree required one year of coursework and no dissertation. Unlike the LLM, which was designed for lawyers with a desire to teach, the MCL was intended for lawyers who planned to practice. The first students graduated with a degree from this program in 1985. Since that time, a certificate in legal studies was also added, which allowed students to take coursework for one semester.

When Fred Aman assumed the deanship in 1991, he placed a new emphasis on globalization and promoted programs and activities to develop global connections.

# YU-CHI "TONY" WANG

Yu-Chi Wang was born in Taipei City, Taiwan (Republic of China) in 1969. After earning his LLB from National Taiwan University, he applied to the IU School of Law's LLM program at the suggestion of one of his professors. Following the completion of the LLM program in 1993, Wang entered the newly established SJD program at the law school, becoming the first student to be awarded the doctor of juridical science degree in 1997. Upon returning to Taiwan, he began his academic career, teaching at the Graduate School of Social Informatics at Yuan-Ze University as well as the Department of Law at Shih-Hsin University, where he became a respected expert in privacy and telecommunications law. Wang joined the Science and Technology Law Center of the Institute for Information Industry in 2005, ultimately becoming the director of the center.

From 2008 to 2016, Wang served in the administration of President Ma Ying-Jeou in a variety of roles including secretary and spokesperson, senior advisor to the National Security Council, and minister of the Mainland Affairs Council. He was the first cabinet member of Taiwan to lead an official delegation to Mainland China since 1949 and was also the first minister of the Mainland Affairs Council to hold official meetings with his Mainland China counterpart. In 2016, Wang returned to the Department of Law at Shih-Hsin University as an associate professor. Yu-Chi Wang was a founding member of the law school's Global Advisory Board and was inducted into the Academy of Law Alumni Fellows in 2018.

FIG. SIDEBAR 6.3. Yu-Chi "Tony" Wang speaking with law students at the Maurer School of Law. November 11, 2015. Photographer: James Boyd. *Maurer School of Law Photo Archive.*

Faculty were encouraged to travel and make new connections with schools and colleagues throughout the world; new programs were developed to allow JD students the opportunity to travel abroad; and new emphasis was placed on growing the graduate legal-studies program. The strengthening of global connections continued through the deanships of Lauren Robel and Austen Parrish.

The law school established the doctor of juridical science (SJD) degree in 1995, receiving ABA approval in 1996. Conceived as a very selective program, this degree was intended to give a few exceptional students the opportunity for extended study, research, and writing. The premise was that candidates for the SJD would already have earned an LLM from a demanding program. One academic year in residence was required, as well as the completion of a doctoral dissertation under the supervision of a faculty committee. The first graduate of the SJD program was Yu-Chi "Tony" Wang, who was awarded the degree in 1997, having also earned the LLM degree from the law school in 1993. While it's still a very selective program, the number of SJD candidates has grown over the years.

Although in existence since 1918, the LLM program remained very small. In response to changes in the market for graduate legal education, the degree requirements were revised in 1999. Previously, candidates had been required to complete a thesis before the LLM was awarded. The revisions created two LLM tracks: one required a thesis for those interested in pursuing a more advanced degree or an academic career and one required only the completion of coursework. Although the LLM thesis-track enrollment remained steady, the nonthesis track grew substantially. In 2016, the program was again changed to allow for specialization. In addition to a general LLM, six specializations were approved: business and commercial law, financial regulation and capital markets, information privacy and cybersecurity law, intellectual property law, international and comparative law and globalization, and American law.

In 2017, the LLM program received an A+ rating from the *International Jurist*. Schools were rated in four categories: academics, law school experience, career planning, and value. Maurer shared A+ honors with other top schools in the country, including Duke, University of Pennsylvania, and University of Minnesota. Maurer was one of only two schools in the United States to receive an A+ in all four categories; Ohio State was the other recipient. The LLM program was selected from 450 programs offered by 153 law schools across the country.

Through the years, the School of Law has offered a limited number of PhD specializations. According to the October 1968 issue of the *Bill of Particulars*, the first proposal, for a PhD in law and economics, was presented in 1968. Currently a PhD in law and democracy is offered through the law school's Center for Constitutional Democracy. Designed to educate students in the way that law structures

**FIG. 6.7.** Annual Socctoberfest soccer match between LLM students and JD students. This has been an annual tradition at Maurer since 2003. October 27, 2016. Photographer: James Boyd. *Maurer School of Law Photo Archive*.

FIG. 6.8. Graduate Legal Studies Program students in 2004–5. *Jerome Hall Law Library Archives 008\2016.LLMGroup.3.*

democracy, the program incorporates not only legal scholarship but also political science, anthropology, and area studies. In addition to coursework and a doctoral dissertation, students complete fieldwork overseas and an internship at the center.

Between 1994 and 2002, the number of new graduate students matriculating increased substantially, from around twenty students to more than sixty each year. For most of its existence, the graduate legal-studies program had been administered through a variety of offices, with no staff assigned exclusively to the program. With the growth in enrollment, more resources were required. Professor Joseph Hoffmann stepped up to serve as the director of international programs from 1998 until 2003, and Professor Lisa Farnsworth served as the director of graduate legal studies from the 1990s until 2016, both dealing primarily with academic issues and recruiting. Enormous administrative tasks to be handled with the growing program prompted the law school, in 2001, to create the position of assistant dean for international programs in order to take responsibility for these programs' nonacademic aspects. Scott Palmer (JD; 2001) served as the first assistant dean,

**FIG. 6.9.** Inaugural Global Advisory Council, in the Federal Room at Indiana Memorial Union. 2017. Photographer: Ann Schertz. *Jerome Hall Law Library Archives 035\2018.EVENTS.5.*

and Lesley Davis succeeded him in 2003. Professor Gabrielle Goodwin assumed the position of director of graduate legal studies in 2016, taking responsibility for the academic aspects of the program.

Beginning in 1904 with the arrival of three students from the Philippines, the IU Maurer School of Law now has graduates from all over the world. The school annually matriculates between sixty-five and seventy-five new graduate students. Although they come from many countries, the largest alumni groups are in China, Korea, Taiwan, and Thailand. In 2016, Dean Austen Parrish announced the formation of the Global Advisory Board to provide advice to the dean in maintaining and improving the school's standing and reputation outside the United States, stating, "These alumni are among our greatest ambassadors, and we hope that this new board will help strengthen ties between the school and our friends throughout the world" ("Plans for Global Advisory Board Announced," *Ergo*, Fall 2016, 29).

FIG. 7.1. Maurer School of Law banner on a snowy day. March 21, 2018. Photographer: James Boyd. *Maurer School of Law Photo Archive.*

# 7 | NOTABLE GRADUATES OF THE MAURER SCHOOL OF LAW

FROM THE BEGINNING, LAW SCHOOL GRADUATES have distinguished themselves through professional and service achievements. Over ten thousand alumni can be found throughout the world, making a difference in the communities where they live. Although it is impossible to honor every deserving person, the law school formally recognizes the accomplishments of its graduates through the Academy of Law Alumni Fellows and the Distinguished Service Award.

The Academy of Law Alumni Fellows was established in 1985 to recognize alumni who have distinguished themselves in their careers through personal

## MAURER GRADUATES IN MEDIA AND SPORTS

Early graduates of the law school frequently held other jobs in addition to practicing law, such as farmer, postmaster, banker, and, often, newspaper editor. Clarendon Davisson, a member of the first graduating class of 1844, practiced law in Petersburg, Indiana, before returning to Bloomington to edit the local newspaper, the *Herald*. After that, he was involved with several other newspapers, including the Indianapolis *Journal*, Chicago *Tribune*, and St. Louis *Democrat*. In 1862, Davisson was appointed Consul at Bordeaux, France. Upon returning, he joined the editorial staff of the New Orleans *Republican*. Other early newspaper editors include John Greer (LLB; 1849), Topeka *Tribune*; Simeon K. Wolfe (LLB; 1850), Corydon *Weekly Democrat*; Daniel M. Baker (LLB; 1861), Chariton *Leader* (Iowa); Orlan F. Baker (LLB; 1864), Vincennes *Times*; and Nathan Ward Fitzgerald (LLB; 1871), Washington, DC, *World*.

More recently graduates have found success in various forms of media. John Onoda (JD; 1976) started out as did many of our early graduates, in the newspaper business, spending five years as a reporter with the Houston *Chronicle*. He then moved into public relations, working for Levi Strauss, General Motors, Visa, and Charles Schwab, before joining Fleischman-Hillard International Communications. Michael S. "Mickey" Maurer (JD; 1967) wears many hats; among them is chairman of the board of the IBJ Corporation, which owns and publishes the *Indiana Business Journal*, *Court and Commercial Record*, and the *Indiana Lawyer*. Randy M. Lebedoff (JD;

FIG. SIDEBAR 7.1A. Rodolfo "Rudy" Chapa Jr. with his family at ceremony inducting him into the Academy of Law Alumni Fellows. April 7, 2017. Photographer: Deborah W. Conkle. *Jerome Hall Law Library Archives 035\2018.EVENT.4–30*.

1975) joined the Star Tribune and Media Company LLC in Minneapolis, where she has served as senior vice president, general counsel, and secretary.

Moving to television, Andrea Morehead (JD; 1996) is an Emmy award–winning journalist. Following law school, she worked at WXIN-TV in Indianapolis and in Grand Rapids as a TV news anchor before returning to Indianapolis in 1999 to become a news anchor for WTHR-TV. Working behind the cameras, Laurie Robinson Haden (JD; 1998) is senior vice president and assistant general counsel of CBS Corporation. She also founded Corporate Counsel Women of Color in 2004, a nonprofit professional organization to advance women-of-color attorneys and to foster diversity in the legal profession.

Since the days of the law-medic sports rivalries, law students have loved sports. Some students came to law school at the conclusion of their collegiate athletic experience, moving on to successful law and business careers. Among them are Glenn Scolnik (JD; 1978), who played college football at IU and professional football for the NFL's Pittsburgh Steelers and New York Giants. He practiced law in Indiana before joining the New York private-equity firm, Hammond, Kennedy, Whitney and Co., eventually becoming chairman of the board. Harry Gonso (JD; 1973), starting quarterback on IU's 1967 Rose Bowl team, joined the Indianapolis law firm Ice Miller, where he became a partner, and also served as chief of staff for Governor Mitch Daniels.

Some former college athletes remained in the sports arena following law school. Rodolfo "Rudy" Chapa Jr. (JD; 1985) achieved All-American status six times in cross-country and track while at the University of Oregon. In 1992, he joined Nike as the global director of sports marketing, eventually leaving to pursue various interests, including founding SPARQ, a sports equipment and media company. Milton Thompson (JD; 1979) was a first-team All-American baseball player at Wittenberg University. Drafted by the Baltimore Orioles, he decided on law school instead. His many successful endeavors include president and CEO of Grand Slam III, LLC, a sports, entertainment, and recreation management-consulting firm.

FIG. SIDEBAR 7.1B. Raphael Prevot Jr. with Attorney General Janet Reno at graduation. Both spoke at the ceremony. 1995. Photographer: Mike Finger. *Jerome Hall Law Library Archives 032\2015.EVENT.190–120.*

It is not necessary to be a college athlete to have a successful career in the sports industry, as David Elmore (JD; 1958) and Raphael Prevot Jr. (JD; 1984) show. Elmore founded the Elmore Sports Group, a successful sports and entertainment conglomerate that owns minor league baseball teams and a hockey team, as well as companies that specialize in travel, facilities management, special events management, and sports marketing. After working in Florida for a few years, Prevot moved to New York City in 1993 to work for the National Football League as the NFL labor-relations counsel, where he represented teams in labor disputes and negotiated collective bargaining agreements between the NFL Management Council and the NFL Players Association. Prevot died in 2008 at the age of forty-nine.

FIG. 7.2. Sherman Minton, US Supreme Court associate justice, 1949–57. Circa 1949. *IU Archives P0042103.*

achievements and dedication to the highest standards of the profession. Through a wide range of professional roles, academy fellows bring honor to the legal profession and enhance the law school's reputation. Induction into the academy is the highest honor the Maurer School of Law bestows upon its graduates. A list of inductees can be found in appendix 3.

Established in 1997, the Distinguished Service Award recognizes graduates who have distinguished themselves in service to their communities and the school in ways far exceeding traditional business, professional, and civic duties. These alumni define the law school's ideals for community service and serve as accomplished role models, not only for the law school but also for the greater community. A list of recipients can be found in appendix 4.

It is impossible to mention all of the deserving individuals who have passed through the law school. They can be found in law firms across the country and, indeed, the world. They are also doing important work in public defender offices, prosecuting attorney offices, nonprofit organizations, and businesses. Others have made their impact in courtrooms, political offices, and classrooms, teaching future generations of students.

Maurer alumni have held judicial appointments on federal and state levels across the country, ranging from local courts to the highest court in the land. Sherman Minton (LLB; 1915) is the only Indiana law graduate appointed to the nation's highest court, serving as associate justice on the US Supreme Court from 1949 until his retirement in 1957. Born in Georgetown, Indiana, in 1890, he graduated from New Albany High School, where he excelled in sports. While an undergraduate at IU, he was a fraternity brother to Paul McNutt and was later a law school classmate of Wendell Willkie. After law school, he attended Yale, receiving an LLM in 1917. Minton practiced law in New Albany until his election to the US Senate in 1934, where he remained until 1940, when President Franklin Roosevelt nominated him to the US Court of Appeals for the Seventh Circuit.

FIG. 7.3. Judge Jesse Eschbach speaking at the law school. April 1993. Photographer: Jim Doyle. *Jerome Hall Law Library Archives 029\2016.EVENT.241–2.*

Nine years later he was nominated to the US Supreme Court by President Truman, where he succeeded Justice Wiley Rutledge, who actually began his legal education at Indiana University but finished at the University of Colorado. Minton was noted for his broad views of government power and his abhorrence of racial segregation. He retired from the court in 1957 and died in 1965.

Like Minton, Walter E. Treanor (LLB; 1922), John S. Hastings (LLB; 1924), Jesse Eschbach (JD; 1949), Michael Kanne (JD; 1968), and John Tinder (JD; 1975) also served on the US Court of Appeals for the Seventh Circuit. Treanor was a member of the law school faculty from the time of his graduation until 1930, when he was appointed to the Indiana Supreme Court. Treanor was nominated to the seventh circuit by President Roosevelt in 1937, serving on the court until his death in 1941. Hastings was nominated by President Eisenhower in 1957 and became chief judge two years later, a role he continued until 1968. Judges Eschbach, Kanne, and Tinder all served on the US district courts for Indiana prior to their appointment.

In fact, fourteen Maurer graduates have served on the US district courts for Indiana, including S. Hugh Dillin (LLB; 1938), appointed to the US District Court

FIG. 7.4. Judges Sue Shields, William I. Garrard, John G. Baker, Linda Chezem, and Ezra H. Friedlander. All served on the Indiana Court of Appeals. 1994. *Jerome Hall Law Library Archives 010\2014.EVENT.18.*

for Southern Indiana in 1961 and best known for his decisions desegregating the Indianapolis public schools. Dillin assumed senior status in 1993, which continued until his death in 2006. Another graduate, Sue Shields (LLB; 1961) was selected to serve as US magistrate for the Southern District of Indiana in 1994, the first woman to hold the position in the district courts of Indiana. Prior to this, from 1978 to 1994, Shields served on the Indiana Court of Appeals, where she was the first woman appointed; she was also the first female trial court judge in Indiana, when she was elected to the Hamilton County Superior Court in 1964. Another graduate, Gonzalo P. Curiel (JD; 1979) was appointed to the US District Court for the Southern District of California by President Obama in 2012. Prior to his appointment, Curiel served as an assistant US attorney in California from 1989 until 2006 and as a San Diego Superior Court judge from 2006 until 2012.

**FIG. 7.5.** Chief Justice Loretta Rush, Justice Christopher Goff, and Justice Geoffrey Slaughter, Indiana Supreme Court. 2017. Photographer: Chris Bucher. *Photo courtesy of Indiana Supreme Court.*

Indiana law graduates have served on all levels of courts in Indiana. To date, twenty have been justices on the Indiana Supreme Court, beginning with Samuel Buskirk (LLB; 1845), a member of the second graduating class who was elected to the Indiana Supreme Court in 1870 and served through 1876. Curtis Grover Shake (LLB; 1910) served on the Indiana Supreme Court from 1937 until 1945. Following this, in 1947, Shake was appointed to the war crimes trials at Nuremburg, Germany. He was the presiding judge in the *IG Farben* case. More recently Loretta Rush (JD; 1983) was appointed to the Indiana Supreme Court in 2012, becoming the chief justice two years later, the first woman to serve in that capacity. Following Rush's appointment, two other Maurer graduates were appointed to the court: Geoffrey Slaughter (JD; 1989), appointed in 2016, and Christopher Goff (JD; 1996), appointed in 2017.

Alumni have served on state courts throughout the country. Among them are Shirley Abrahamson (JD; 1956), who was appointed to the Wisconsin Supreme Court in 1976, the first woman to serve on that court. In 1996 she became chief

From the time of their arrival, Maurer students are imbued with a sense of social responsibility and the importance of helping those who do not have the ability or resources to help themselves. Through their professional careers and community service, alumni have committed themselves to this cause. The following are but a few examples of their extraordinary work.

Harriet Bouslog (LLB; 1936) devoted her career as a labor lawyer and civil rights activist to defending the rights of Hawaiian laborers, becoming a champion for the working class. She represented the International Longshore and Warehouse Union (ILWU), fighting for fair labor laws and wages for Hawaiians. Her handling of the appeal for two indigent Hawaiians convicted of murder is largely credited with ending the death penalty in Hawaii in 1957. When defending the Hawaii Seven, who were charged as being communist conspirators, Bouslog found herself to be the subject of a lawsuit after she was disbarred for making public comments about the case. She was ultimately reinstated after the landmark US Supreme Court case *In re Sawyer*, 360 US 622 (1959), which affirmed the rights of an attorney to speak openly and freely within the bounds of ethics. She died in 1998 in Hawaii.

Jeff Richardson (JD; 1977) spent most of his career helping people afflicted with HIV/AIDS worldwide. As part of these efforts, he served as executive director of GMHC, the largest AIDS service organization in the United States, and as vice president of the Abbott Fund, a global

FIG. SIDEBAR 7.2A. Harriet Bouslog with US Supreme Court Chief Justice William H. Rehnquist (*left*) and her husband, Stephen Sawyer (*right*), at the law school dedication. September 12, 1986. *Jerome Hall Law Library Archives 010\2014.EVENT.6.*

health care nonprofit, overseeing its efforts to help children affected by HIV/AIDS in the developing world. Elizabeth Shuman-Moore (JD; 1982) devoted her career to public interest work. Shuman-Moore served for seventeen years as director of the Hate Crimes Project of the Chicago Lawyers' Committee for Civil Rights, advocating for hate crimes victims. Following that, she served as director of the Chicago Lawyers' Committee's Fair Housing Project, working to eliminate housing discrimination and representing residents who need assistance in enforcing their fair housing rights.

Another 1982 graduate, Jane Raley, devoted her professional life to helping those in need. She worked at the Illinois Office of the State Appellate Defender, representing indigent felony defendants on appeal, and was the senior staff attorney at the Capital Resource Center, where her practice was devoted solely to death penalty work. Following that, she was the codirector of the Center for Wrongful Convictions at Northwestern University School of Law for fourteen years, until her death in December 2014. A passionate advocate for the falsely accused, Raley was instrumental in the exoneration of eleven inmates from prison. As a result of her dedication, many inmates called her Saint Jane.

Many alumni have performed extraordinary acts of service outside their professional work. Jean McGrew Stoffregen (JD; 1942) was one of the few women to work on the Nuremberg Trials. In 1947, Indiana Supreme Court Justice Frank Richman asked Stoffregen to assist him at the trials. While there, she traveled throughout Europe helping those displaced by the war with emigration documentation and processing. Upon returning to the United States, she continued to help refugees and immigrants rebuild their lives. Arthur Lopez (JD; 1983) had a stellar law career in Washington, DC, but he wanted to do more to help children growing up at risk. A certified USA swim coach, Lopez founded Nadar Por Vida (Swimming for Life), a nonprofit organization committed to giving minority and low-income children a taste of

FIG. SIDEBAR 7.2B. Arthur Lopez with Donna Wilbur Fromm at the Academy of Law Alumni Fellows ceremony. April 17, 2015. Photographer: Deborah W. Conkle. *Maurer School of Law Photo Archive.*

competitive swimming. While teaching the kids to swim, Lopez instilled in them the importance of education and responsible citizenship. Lowell E. Baier (JD; 1964) has been a tireless advocate for natural resources and wildlife conservation, while also running a successful business. Baier has received numerous awards for his advocacy, including Conservationist of the Year by the National Fish and Wildlife Foundation as well as *Outdoor Life*, and in 2017, he received the Rose Award for distinguished service to the Theodore Roosevelt Association.

justice, a position she held until 2015. Born in West Virginia, Franklin Cleckley (JD; 1965) came to Indiana to pursue higher education. Following a stint with the Navy Judge Advocate General Corps, he taught at the West Virginia College of Law, as the school's first African American faculty member. After twenty-five years of teaching, he was appointed to the West Virginia Supreme Court of Appeals in 1994, where he was the first African American justice on the court. After two years, Cleckley returned to teaching.

Juanita Kidd Stout, who received a JD in 1948 and LLM in 1954, was born in Oklahoma in 1919. She graduated from high school at sixteen and earned a college degree from the University of Iowa in 1939, when few African Americans had the opportunity to pursue higher education. After teaching high school in Oklahoma, she came to IU with her husband, who was attending graduate school. Desiring to become a lawyer, she completed two law degrees while in Bloomington. After practicing law in Philadelphia, Stout was elected judge of the Philadelphia Municipal Court in 1959, becoming the first African American woman to be elected judge in the United States. She achieved another first when, in 1988, she was appointed to the Pennsylvania Supreme Court, becoming the first African American woman to serve on a state supreme court. Stout stepped down after one year, having met the mandatory retirement age of seventy, and returned to the Common Pleas Court, where she remained until her death in 1998.

Political office has been a calling for many Maurer graduates, from statehouses to the halls of Congress. Willis A. Gorman (LLB; 1845) was the second territorial governor of Minnesota, holding office from 1853 until 1857. He previously served in the Indiana legislature and was a member of the US House of Representatives from 1849 until 1853. A supporter of Franklin Pierce for president, he was rewarded with the governorship when Pierce won the election. At the end of his appointment, Gorman remained in Minnesota, practicing law in St. Paul and serving in the state legislature. Arthur C. Mellette (LLB; 1866) practiced law in Muncie, Indiana, following graduation, where he was elected to the Indiana legislature, purchased the *Muncie Times* newspaper, and served as county superintendent of schools. He moved his family west to the Dakota Territory in search of a better climate for his wife's failing health. Mellette became a prosperous attorney and leading citizen in his new home and was an early proponent of statehood for the territory. In March 1889, he was appointed governor of the Dakota Territory by President Benjamin Harrison. When the territory was divided later that same year, he was elected as the first governor of South Dakota, serving from 1889 until 1893.

In Indiana, over two hundred graduates have served in the Indiana General Assembly, and two have been elected governor. George Craig (LLB; 1932) was

**FIG. 7.6.** Judge Juanita Kidd Stout with Daniel James (*left*), James Thornburg (*immediate right*), and Dean Bryant Garth (*far right*). They were attending the law school building dedication and were inducted into the Academy of Law Alumni Fellows. September 1986. *Jerome Hall Law Library Archives 009\2014.BUILD.1–90.*

governor from 1953 until 1957, and Frank O'Bannon (JD; 1957) served from 1997 until his death in 2003. While serving in the army during World War II, Craig became acquainted with General Eisenhower, who influenced his thinking on political issues. Returning to Indiana, he was active in the American Legion, becoming the national commander in 1949. This sparked his political ambitions, and he was elected governor in spite of his differences with the more conservative state Republication Party. After leaving office, Craig practiced law in Virginia, returning to Indiana upon his retirement. O'Bannon practiced law in Corydon, Indiana, and was the publisher of the *Corydon Democrat* following law school. In 1970, he was elected to the Indiana state senate and worked his way up the state political ladder, serving as lieutenant governor during Evan Bayh's administration,

**FIG. 7.7.** Birch Bayh during his time as a law student, standing on the steps of the law school. January 16, 1958. Photographer: Jim Hanning. *IU Archives P0035978.*

before his election as governor in 1996. O'Bannon suffered a massive stroke in Chicago while attending an international trade conference in 2003 and died five days later.

A number of graduates have been elected to the US Congress. Four have served as US senators: Sherman Minton, William Jenner, Vance Hartke, and Birch Bayh. Minton was elected to the US Senate in 1934, prior to his appointment to the Seventh Circuit Court of Appeals. William Jenner (LLB; 1932) was elected to the Indiana state senate in 1934, where he rose through the Republican leadership ranks before resigning to join the Army Air Corps in 1942. After his discharge in 1944, he was elected to the US Senate, where he remained until 1958, when he chose not to run for reelection and instead returned to his law practice and business interests in southern Indiana. Vance Hartke (LLB; 1948) served as mayor of Evansville, Indiana, from 1956 until he was elected to the US Senate in 1958, assuming the seat held by Jenner. He served in the Senate for eighteen years, until losing his seat to Richard Lugar in 1976. After leaving the Senate, Hartke practiced law in the Washington, DC, area.

Birch Bayh (JD; 1960) was already serving in the Indiana legislature while attending law school, having been elected to the House of Representatives in 1954. In 1962, at only thirty-four years old, he was elected to the US Senate and served for eighteen years, until losing his bid for reelection in 1980. During those years, he became one of the most influential politicians to come out of Indiana. Bayh was the author of two constitutional amendments: the Twenty-Fifth Amendment, establishing presidential succession, and the Twenty-Sixth Amendment, lowering the voting age to eighteen. Additionally, he was author of Title IX of the Higher Education Act of 1965, mandating equal opportunities for women in educational institutions that receive federal funding; was author and cosponsor of the Bayh-Dole Act that enabled universities and small businesses to gain ownership of federally funded copyrights; was the architect for the Juvenile Justice Act; and was chairman of the Senate Select Committee on Intelligence. Following his time in the Senate, Bayh practiced law in the Washington, DC, area, served on numerous boards, and continued to advocate for causes such as Title IX and the direct election of the president. Bayh's eldest son, Evan, served Indiana as secretary of state, governor, and US senator.

To date, more than twenty-five graduates have represented Indiana as members of the US House of Representatives. The earliest, Willis A. Gorman (LLB; 1845) was in the House of Representatives from 1849 until 1854. Among the longest serving and most influential were Charles Halleck (LLB; 1924) and Lee Hamilton (JD; 1956). Charles Halleck was elected to the US House of Representatives in 1935 and served for thirty-four years, until his retirement in 1969. During his

FIG. 7.8. Commencement speaker Lee Hamilton receiving an honorary degree at IU commencement. May 4, 1991. Photographer: Jerry Mitchell. *Jerome Hall Law Library Archives 023\2015.ALUM.3–3.*

tenure, he held leadership positions in the Republican Party, including house majority leader and house minority leader. Committed to civil rights, Halleck worked hard to obtain Republican votes to pass the Civil Rights Act of 1964. After his retirement, he returned to Rensselaer, Indiana.

Lee Hamilton was elected to the US House of Representatives in 1964, where he served for thirty-four years. During his years in Congress, Hamilton, a Democrat, was widely respected by both parties for his knowledge of foreign affairs. After leaving the House, Hamilton continued to be an active participant in the important issues facing the country. He became director of the Woodrow Wilson International Center for Scholars in Washington, DC, and established the Center on Congress at Indiana University. He served as a member of the US Commission on National Security in the Twenty-First Century (Hart-Rudman Commission), was chair with Howard Baker of the Baker-Hamilton Commission to Investigate Certain Security Issues at Los Alamos, was appointed to the advisory council to the US Department of Homeland Security, and served as vice-chair of the National Commission on Security Attacks Upon the United States (9/11 Commission).

To date, no Maurer graduate has been elected president of the United States. Coming close, Wendell Willkie (LLB; 1916) was nominated to head the Republican ticket in 1940, ultimately losing the election to Franklin D. Roosevelt (FDR), who ran for a third term. Born in Elwood, Indiana, in 1892, Willkie was known as a campus radical during his undergraduate years at IU, where Paul McNutt was a friend and political ally. After completing law school, he practiced for a short time in Elwood before joining the army. Upon his return, Willkie practiced law

**FIG. 7.9.** Wendell Willkie, 1940 Republican candidate for president of the United States. Circa 1940. *Photo by Philippe Halsman © Halsman Archive.*

in Akron, Ohio, and then New York City. In 1933, after serving as its general counsel, he became the president of Commonwealth and Southern Corporation, the nation's largest utilities holding company.

Although a lifelong Democrat, his opposition to much of Roosevelt's New Deal legislation caused Willkie to join the Republican Party. His rise to the national ticket was meteoric, considering that he had never held political office and was a former Democrat. Following the election in 1940, Willkie and FDR became unlikely political allies, primarily because of their similar views on civil rights and foreign policy. He traveled overseas as the president's personal representative, observing the war and meeting with foreign leaders. In 1943, Willkie wrote *One World*, an immensely popular book that called for international peacekeeping after the war. At home, he was a strong advocate for the rights of African Americans, calling for improved housing, education, and health care. Willkie, who died in 1944 after suffering several heart attacks, may never have become president, but he secured a lasting place in history. As an aside, McNutt was a hopeful for the Democrat nomination in 1940 if Roosevelt decided not to run for a third term. That would have set up an interesting situation for the old friends from their days at Indiana University. With FDR's decision, that conflict was averted.

A number of alumni have distinguished themselves as academicians. During the late nineteenth and early twentieth centuries it was not unusual for alumni to teach at the law school, generally for short periods of time. After World War II, fewer graduates were hired for the permanent teaching faculty. A notable exception was Val Nolan (JD; 1949), who joined the law faculty immediately upon his graduation and remained until his retirement in 1985. Not only did he have a remarkable law career, but Nolan was also a world-renowned ornithologist, holding a joint appointment with the biology department for many years. He continued to teach

FIG. 7.10. Mickey Maurer, Val Nolan, and Lauren Robel at the Val Nolan Faculty Chair inaugural lecture. The chair was established by Mickey and Janie Maurer to honor Val Nolan, and Lauren Robel was the first recipient. March 31, 2000. Photographer: Kip May. *Jerome Hall Law Library Archives 019\2015.EVENT.103–7.*

and research long after his official retirement. Julia Lamber (JD; 1972) joined the faculty in 1979, where she served with distinction until her retirement in 2013. A nationally recognized authority on Title IX, she also served the university in numerous administrative capacities, including dean of the Office of Women's Affairs.

Four alumni members of the faculty have served as dean, beginning with the first dean, David D. Banta (LLB; 1857), who served from 1889 until his death in 1896. William Rogers (LLB; 1892) was appointed to succeed him, remaining until 1902, when he left for the deanship at the University of Cincinnati Law School. Leon Wallace (LLB; 1933) was the third alumnus to become dean. He was a member of the faculty from 1945 until his retirement in 1976, serving as dean from 1952 until 1966. Lauren K. Robel (JD; 1983) joined the School of Law faculty in 1985 and was appointed dean in 2003, after first serving as interim dean. The first woman to serve as dean, she remained so until 2012, when she was appointed provost for the Bloomington campus and executive vice president for the university.

FIG. 7.11. George P. Smith II, Judge John Tinder, Linda Chezem, V. William Hunt, and Milt Thompson at the ceremony inducting them into the Academy of Law Alumni Fellows. April 2007. *Jerome Hall Law Library 014\2015.EVENT.29–32.*

Alumni have distinguished themselves at other law schools and universities across the country, as well as abroad. Among them are J. Keith Mann (LLB; 1949), who was on the faculty at the Stanford Law School from 1952 until his retirement in 1988 and is credited as one of the people to make Stanford a top law school. Co-incidentally, Mann's brother, W. Howard Mann, was a faculty member at the IU law school from 1946 to 1967. Laura J. Cooper (JD; 1974) joined the faculty at the University of Minnesota Law School in 1975, where she became the first woman to receive tenure. Also graduating in 1974, Martha West spent her teaching career at University of California Davis Law School, where she served as associate dean and clinical director, and created the Family Protection and Legal Assistance Clinic. George P. Smith II (JD; 1964) spent most of his teaching career at Catholic University's Columbus School of Law, where he became an internationally recognized scholar on law and health care, specifically bioethics and health law. Kellye Testy

FIG. 7.12. Justice Flerida Ruth Romero with Dean Fred Aman following a lecture given by Justice Romero. September 1994. Photographer: Mark Simons. *Jerome Hall Law Library Archives 029\2016.EVENT.213–2.*

(JD; 1991) joined the faculty at Seattle University Law School in 1992, becoming its first female dean in 2005. In 2009, she became the first female dean at the University of Washington School of Law, a position she held until stepping down in 2017 to become the president and CEO of the Law School Admission Council.

Some graduates have pursued academia outside the law school realm. Following a successful thirty-year career at Eli Lilly and Co, Alecia DeCoudreaux (JD; 1978) became president of Mills College in 2011, where she remained until her retirement in 2016. Jost Delbrück (LLM; 1960) and Jorge Bocobo (LLB; 1907) both became presidents of universities in their respective countries. Delbrück served as president of the University of Kiel in Germany, and Bocobo was president of the University of the Philippines. Flerida Ruth P. Romero (LLM; 1955) was one of the most prominent scholar-lawyers in Philippine history. She began her academic career at the University of the Philippines in the Labor Education Center

**FIG. 7.13.** Hoagy Carmichael playing piano at the Indiana Memorial Union. November 1946. *IU Archives P0043597.*

and later was a professor of law at the same institution. Romero was the guiding force behind the establishment of the Asian Labor Education Center, which later became the School of Labor and Industrial Relations. She was responsible for drafting many pieces of legislation, most prominently the Family Code of 1987. To help the Filipino people better understand the law, Romero wrote a newspaper column and hosted a radio call-in show. In 1986, she was chosen to oversee the

**FIG. 7.14.** Michael Uslan revealing his Superman shirt following the law school commencement ceremony. May 8, 1976. *IU Archives P0043031.*

creation of a new Philippine constitution, which established democracy and ended the dictatorship of Ferdinand Marcos. From 1991 until 1999, she served as a justice of the Supreme Court of the Philippines. Romero died in 2017.

Finally, any mention of notable graduates must include two who made their careers in the world of entertainment: Hoagy Carmichael (LLB; 1926) and Michael Uslan (JD; 1976). Carmichael was born in Bloomington in 1899. His love for music came from his mother, who played piano at local dances and silent movies, and he frequently tagged along. After entering Indiana University, he developed a passion for jazz, forming his own group, Carmichael's Collegians, who traveled throughout Indiana and Ohio. After graduating from law school, he moved to Florida, where he was a law clerk for a short time before returning to practice law in Indianapolis. This did not last long, and he happily gave up law for music. During his musical career, Carmichael wrote hundreds of songs, including "Star Dust," "Georgia on My Mind," "Heart and Soul," "Lazy River," and "In the Cool, Cool, Cool of the Evening," for which he won an Oscar. He eventually moved into acting and appeared in a number of movies and TV shows. He was inducted into the Songwriters Hall of Fame in 1971. Carmichael died in California in 1981, and his body was returned to his native Bloomington for burial.

Michael Uslan, born in Bayonne, New Jersey, in 1951, had a boyhood dream to write Batman comics. While an undergraduate at IU, he taught the first accredited college course on comic books, which led DC Comics to invite him to write a Batman comic. Following law school, he became a production attorney for United Artists, eventually acquiring the rights to Batman. Uslan began a quest to bring the dark, serious Batman from the comics to the big screen, a journey which took a decade. Finally, in 1989, *Batman* was released by Warner Brothers and became the highest-grossing movie of the year. Uslan, president of Branded Entertainment, has produced many successful movies and series and has written more than thirty books.

FIG APPENDIX 1.1. IU logo in limestone on the south patio of Baier Hall. July 22, 2013. Photographer: Ann Schertz. *Maurer School of Law Photo Archive*.

# *Time Line*

| | |
|---|---|
| **1835** | Indiana University Board of Trustees pass a resolution to create law professorship. |
| **1838** | Indiana General Assembly changes the name of Indiana College to Indiana University, adding the study of law and medicine to its mission. |
| **1842** | On December 5, 1842, David McDonald delivers the inaugural lecture, marking the official beginning of the Indiana University School of Law. |
| **1844** | Law department graduates first class of five students. |
| **1877** | Although successful, the law department is suspended by the trustees, primarily due to financial difficulties of the university. |
| **1889** | School of Law reopens, and David D. Banta is named as first dean. |
| **1890** | Law school is located in Library Hall (later to be named Maxwell Hall). |
| **1892** | Tamar Althouse becomes the first woman to graduate from the law school. |
| **1895** | Law school moves to Kirkwood Hall. |
| **1896** | William Perry Rogers is named the second dean, following death of David Banta. |
| **1900** | Association of American Law Schools forms; the law school is one of thirty-two charter members. |
| **1901** | Growing school moves once again, to the third floor of Wylie Hall. In the same year, the course of study increases from two to three years. |
| **1902** | George L. Reinhard is named the third dean of the School of Law. |
| **1904** | First international students arrive from the Philippines. |
| **1905** | Masuji Miyakawa becomes the first Asian American graduate. |
| **1906** | Enoch G. Hogate named the fourth dean. |

**1907** Jorge Bocobo, Francisco Delgado, and Mariano H. de Joya become the first international students to graduate.

**1908** Law school moves to Maxwell Hall, after the new library building is completed.

**1909** Samuel S. Dargan becomes first the African American graduate.

**1917** JD degree is established. Roscoe O'Byrne and William Seagle become the first recipients in 1918.

**1918** Charles M. Hepburn is named the fifth dean. LLM degree is established, and Felino Lorenzo Merced becomes the first recipient. Program remains very small until latter part of the twentieth century.

**1921** ABA establishes standards for law schools. Indiana Law receives Class A standing in 1923, one of only thirty-nine law schools to receive this honor.

**1925** Paul V. McNutt is named the sixth dean, at thirty-five years old, the youngest in the law school's history. Rowena Compton is hired as the first law librarian.

**1926** First issue of the *Indiana Law Journal* is published.

**1932** Dean McNutt is elected governor of Indiana.

**1933** Bernard C. Gavit is named the seventh dean.

**1944** Indiana Law School in Indianapolis merges with IU Law as Evening Division.

**1952** Leon H. Wallace is named the eighth dean.

**1956** Law school moves from Maxwell Hall to the new Law Building.

**1957** Dedication of the new Law Building. US Supreme Court Chief Justice Earl Warren attends.

**1964** Law faculty establishes the Visiting Committee, later named Board of Visitors.

**1966** William Burnett Harvey is named the ninth dean, the first dean to be hired from outside the law faculty.

**1968** JD becomes the standard degree awarded.

**1969** Indianapolis Division becomes fully autonomous, changes its name to IU School of Law–Indianapolis.

**1972** Douglass G. Boshkoff is named the tenth dean.

1975   "Blue ribbon" panel on legal education in Indiana, appointed by President Ryan, recommends that the IU law schools in Bloomington and Indianapolis remain separate.

1977   Sheldon Jay Plager is named the eleventh dean.

1982   After receiving funding from the state legislature, ground-breaking is held for the law school addition.

1985   Morris S. Arnold is named the twelfth dean.

1986   Building addition and renovation are completed, and the dedication is held in the fall. US Supreme Court Justice William Rehnquist is the featured speaker.

1987   Bryant G. Garth is named the thirteenth dean. The Law and Society Center is launched.

1991   Alfred C. Aman Jr. is named the fourteenth dean.

1992   *Indiana Journal of Global Legal Studies* launches.

1995   SJD degree is approved.

1997   Yu-Chi "Tony" Wang is the first SJD recipient.

2003   Lauren K. Robel is named the fifteenth dean; she is the first female dean.

2007   Law school receives a Lilly grant of $25 million to recruit and retain faculty.

2008   Law School is renamed the Michael Maurer School of Law in recognition of the $35 million gift from Michael S. "Mickey" and Janie Maurer.

2014   Austen L. Parrish is named the sixteenth dean, following Lauren Robel's appointment as provost of the Bloomington campus and vice president of the university.

2015   Law building is renamed Baier Hall, and the law library is renamed Jerome Hall Law Library in recognition of the $20 million gift from Lowell E. Baier.

FIG APPENDIX 2.1. "School of Law" etched into limestone above entrance to Baier Hall. October 17, 2014. Photographer: James Boyd. *Maurer School of Law Photo Archive*.

# *Law School Leaders*
### *1842–*

## Department of Law, 1842–77

| | |
|---|---|
| 1842–53 | David McDonald |
| 1853–57 | James Hughes |
| 1857–61 | James R. M. Bryant |
| 1861–70 | George A. Bicknell |
| 1870–72 | Samuel E. Perkins* |
| 1872–73 | Delana R. Eckles* |
| 1873–74 | David W. LaFollette* |
| 1874–77 | Cyrus F. McNutt* |

* Baskin E. Rhoads also served as professor during the period from 1870 until the department closed in 1877.

## School of Law Deans, 1889–

| | |
|---|---|
| 1889–96 | David D. Banta |
| 1896–1902 | William Perry Rogers |
| 1902–6 | George L. Reinhard |
| 1906–18 | Enoch G. Hogate |
| 1918–25 | Charles M. Hepburn |
| 1925–33 | Paul V. McNutt |
| 1933–51 | Bernard C. Gavit |
| 1952–66 | Leon H. Wallace |
| 1966–71 | William Burnett Harvey |
| 1972–76 | Douglass G. Boshkoff |
| 1977–84 | Sheldon Jay Plager |

| | |
|---|---|
| **1985** | Morris S. Arnold |
| **1987–90** | Bryant G. Garth |
| **1991–2002** | Alfred C. Aman Jr. |
| **2003–12** | Lauren K. Robel |
| **2014–** | Austen Parrish |

FIG APPENDIX 3.1. Academy of Law Alumni Fellows display in Baier Hall. September 9, 2016. Photographer: James Boyd. *Maurer School of Law Photo Archive.*

# *Academy of Law Alumni*
# *Fellows Recipients*
## *1985–2019*

| | | |
|---|---|---|
| SHIRLEY S. ABRAHAMSON | JD | 1956 |
| TERRILL D. ALBRIGHT | JD | 1965 |
| ELLIS B. ANDERSON | JD | 1952 |
| K. EDWIN APPLEGATE | LLB | 1948 |
| LOWELL E. BAIER | JD | 1964 |
| BIRCH BAYH | JD | 1960 |
| ROBERT B. BENSON | JD | 1954 |
| JOSEPH B. BOARD JR. | JD | 1958 |
| JORGE C. BOCOBO | LLB | 1907 |
| SARA S. BOSCO | JD | 1983 |
| HARRIET BOUSLOG | LLB | 1936 |
| SANFORD M. BROOK | JD | 1974 |
| KATHLEEN A. BUCK | JD | 1973 |
| JOSEPH T. BUMBLEBURG | JD | 1961 |
| STEPHEN F. BURNS | JD | 1968 |
| DAVID L. CARDEN | JD | 1976 |
| HOAGLAND "HOAGY" CARMICHAEL | LLB | 1926 |
| WILLARD Z. CARR | JD | 1950 |
| JOHN L. CARROLL | JD | 1948 |
| RICHARD E. CARTER | LLB | 1961 |
| RODOLFO CHAPA JR. | JD | 1985 |
| LINDA L. CHEZEM | JD | 1971 |

| | | |
|---|---|---|
| JOHN W. CHRISTENSEN | JD | 1939 |
| FRANKLIN D. CLECKLEY | JD | 1965 |
| CATHERINE A. CONWAY | JD | 1978 |
| LAURA J. COOPER | JD | 1974 |
| GEORGE CRAIG | LLB | 1932 |
| GONZALO P. CURIEL | JD | 1979 |
| THEODORE R. DANN | JD | 1930 |
| SAMUEL S. DARGAN | LLB | 1909 |
| ALECIA A. DECOUDREAUX | JD | 1978 |
| ANN M. DELANEY | JD | 1977 |
| JOST W. DELBRÜCK | LLM | 1960 |
| PAUL J. DEVAULT | JD | 1932 |
| S. HUGH DILLIN | LLB | 1938 |
| FRANCINA DLOUHY | JD | 1977 |
| DONALD P. DORFMAN | JD | 1957 |
| C. BENJAMIN DUTTON | LLB | 1940 |
| J. LESLIE DUVALL | LLB | 1949 |
| ROBERT P. DUVIN | JD | 1961 |
| FREDERICK F. EICHHORN JR. | JD | 1957 |
| DAVID G. ELMORE | JD | 1958 |
| EWING RABB EMISON | JD | 1950 |
| JESSE E. ESCHBACH | JD | 1949 |
| SIDNEY D. ESKENAZI | JD | 1953 |
| PENELOPE S. FARTHING | JD | 1970 |
| STEPHEN L. FERGUSON | JD | 1966 |
| THOMAS G. FISHER | LLB | 1965 |
| JAMES F. FITZPATRICK | JD | 1959 |
| EUGENE D. FLETCHALL | JD | 1934 |
| DOROTHY J. FRAPWELL | JD | 1973 |
| EZRA H. FRIEDLANDER | LLB | 1965 |

*LEONARD D. FROMM

| | | |
|---|---|---|
| WILLIAM I. GARRARD | JD | 1959 |
| PHILIP C. GENETOS | JD | 1977 |
| CARL M. GRAY | LLB | 1961 |
| CHARLES A. HALLECK | LLB | 1924 |
| LEE H. HAMILTON | JD | 1956 |
| BERNARD HARROLD | LLB | 1951 |
| RUSSELL H. HART JR. | JD | 1956 |
| JOHN S. HASTINGS | LLB | 1924 |
| HOWARD R. HAWKINS | JD | 1941 |
| JOSEPH A. "ANDY" HAYS | LLB | 1959 |
| HUBERT HICKAM | LLB | 1913 |
| WILLIS HICKAM | LLB | 1918 |
| ELWOOD H. HILLIS | JD | 1952 |
| LEROY W. HOFMANN | JD | 1958 |
| JOHN W. HOUGHTON | JD | 1942 |
| V. WILLIAM HUNT | JD | 1969 |
| R. NEIL IRWIN | JD | 1971 |
| DANIEL JAMES | JD | 1929 |
| PAUL G. JASPER | LLB | 1932 |
| MICHAEL S. KANNE | JD | 1968 |
| ROBERT P. KASSING | JD | 1964 |
| BARBARA J. KELLEY | JD | 1973 |
| JOHN F. KIMBERLING | JD | 1950 |
| STEPHEN O. KINNARD | JD | 1972 |
| EARL W. KINTNER | JD | 1938 |
| JULIA LAMBER | JD | 1972 |
| MARY NOLD LARIMORE | JD | 1980 |
| WILLIAM C. LAWRENCE | JD | 1979 |
| THOMAS R. LEMON | JD | 1966 |

| | | |
|---|---|---|
| ELLIOTT D. LEVIN | JD | 1966 |
| THOMAS M. LOFTON | JD | 1954 |
| ROBERT A. LONG | JD | 1971 |
| ARTHUR M. LOTZ | LLB | 1965 |
| ROBERT A. LUCAS | JD | 1949 |
| LARRY A. MACKEY | JD | 1976 |
| J. KEITH MANN | LLB | 1949 |
| MICHAEL S. "MICKEY" MAURER | JD | 1967 |
| FRANCIS X. MCCLOSKEY | JD | 1971 |
| WARREN E. MCGILL | JD | 1945 |
| ROBERT H. MCKINNEY | JD | 1952 |
| RUFUS W. MCKINNEY | JD | 1956 |
| R. BRUCE MCLEAN | JD | 1971 |
| PATRICIA A. MCNAGNY | JD | 1951 |
| WILLIAM F. MCNAGNY | LLB | 1947 |
| CYNTHIA A. METZLER | JD | 1974 |
| JEANNE SEIDEL MILLER | JD | 1948 |
| LLOYD H. MILLIKEN JR. | JD | 1960 |
| SHERMAN MINTON | LLB | 1915 |
| MASUJI MIYAKAWA | LLB | 1905 |
| MARYANN M. MUKETE | JD | 1974 |
| VAL NOLAN JR. | JD | 1949 |
| FRANK L. O'BANNON | JD | 1957 |
| JOSEPH D. O'CONNOR | JD | 1978 |
| JOHN C. ONODA | JD | 1976 |
| ROGER L. PARDIECK | JD | 1963 |
| STEPHEN H. PAUL | JD | 1972 |
| COLLEEN K. PAUWELS | JD | 1986 |
| RAPHAEL M. PREVOT JR. | JD | 1984 |
| JANE E. RALEY | JD | 1982 |

| | | |
|---|---|---|
| JEANETTE F. REIBMAN | JD | 1940 |
| RONALD S. REINSTEIN | JD | 1973 |
| RICHARD S. RHODES | LLB | 1953 |
| JOHN F. "JEFF" RICHARDSON | JD | 1977 |
| JAMES G. RICHMOND | JD | 1969 |
| CLARINE NARDI RIDDLE | JD | 1974 |
| WILLIAM R. RIGGS | JD | 1963 |
| LAUREN K. ROBEL | JD | 1983 |
| FLERIDA RUTH P. ROMERO | LLM | 1955 |
| JOEL ROSENBLOOM | JD | 1954 |
| J. EDWARD ROUSH | JD | 1949 |
| LORETTA H. RUSH | JD | 1983 |
| TAMAR ALTHOUSE SCHOLZ | LLB | 1892 |
| GLENN SCOLNIK | JD | 1978 |
| ZALDWAYNAKA L. "Z" SCOTT | JD | 1983 |
| FRANK SEALES JR. | JD | 1974 |
| V. SUE SHIELDS | LLB | 1961 |
| JACQUELINE A. SIMMONS | JD | 1979 |
| SARAH M. SINGLETON | JD | 1974 |
| GEORGE P. SMITH II | JD | 1964 |
| HUGO "CHAD" SONGER | LLB | 1960 |
| MILTON R. STEWART | JD | 1971 |
| WILLIAM R. STEWART | JD | 1959 |
| THOMAS L. STEVENS | JD | 1955 |
| JUANITA KIDD STOUT | JD | 1948; LLM 1954 |
| VIOLA J. TALIAFERRO | JD | 1977 |
| MILTON O. THOMPSON | JD | 1979 |
| JAMES F. THORNBURG | JD | 1936 |
| JOHN D. TINDER | JD | 1975 |
| DENICE M. TORRES | JD | 1984 |

| | | |
|---|---|---|
| WALTER TREANOR | LLB | 1922 |
| MICHAEL E. USLAN | JD | 1976 |
| CARL E. VER BEEK | JD | 1962 |
| JOSE H. VILLARREAL | JD | 1979 |
| JOHN L. WALDA | JD | 1975 |
| YU-CHI "TONY" WANG | LLM | 1993; SJD 1997 |
| MARTHA S. WEST | JD | 1974 |
| CHARLES WHISTLER | LLB | 1951 |
| WENDELL WILLKIE | LLB | 1916 |

*Only nonalumnus inducted into Academy of Law Alumni Fellows. Served as associate dean for students and alumni relations from 1979 until his death in February 2013.

FIG APPENDIX 4.1. Distinguished Service Award programs. 2017. Photographer: James Boyd. *Maurer School of Law Photo Archive.*

# *Distinguished Service Awards Recipients*

## *1997–2018*

| | | |
|---|---|---|
| ROBERT D. ARONSON | JD | 1976 |
| LOWELL E. BAIER | JD | 1964 |
| M. SCOTT BASSETT | JD | 1986 |
| ROBIN BOLES | JD | 1979 |
| JAMES BROTHERSON | JD | 1978 |
| ANDREW B. BUROKER | JD | 1989 |
| SUSAN K. CARPENTER | JD | 1976 |
| GREGORY A. CASTANIAS | JD | 1990 |
| LYNN H. COYNE | JD | 1972 |
| JEFFREY S. DAVIDSON | JD | 1973 |
| GARY L. DAVIS | JD | 1982 |
| DONALD P. DORFMAN | JD | 1957 |
| MILES C. GERBERDING | LLB | 1956 |
| FRED H. GREGORY | LLB | 1953 |
| JOHN M. HAMILTON | JD | 1986 |
| JANE HENEGAR | JD | 1988 |
| LEROY W. HOFMANN | JD | 1958 |
| JOSEPH H. HOGSETT | JD | 1981 |
| MARK E. HOLCOMB | JD | 1987 |
| FEISAL A. ISTRABADI | JD | 1988 |
| GREGORY J. JORDAN | JD | 1984 |
| JEFFREY J. KENNEDY | JD | 1967 |

| | | |
|---|---|---|
| EDWARD C. KING | JD | 1964 |
| ABIGAIL L. KUZMA | JD | 1981 |
| RANDY M. LEBEDOFF | JD | 1975 |
| CHRISTOPHER D. LEE | JD | 1993 |
| SANDRA LEEK | JD | 1979 |
| FRED J. LOGAN JR. | JD | 1977 |
| ROBERT A. LONG | JD | 1971 |
| ARTHUR A. LOPEZ | JD | 1983 |
| THOMAS YUNLONG MAN | JD | 1997 |
| HOLIDAY HART MCKIERNAN | JD | 1983 |
| LISA C. MCKINNEY | JD | 1992 |
| MARTIN MONTES | JD | 1995 |
| JERRY MOSS | JD | 1962 |
| LINDY G. MOSS | LLB | 1952 |
| SUSAN B. NOYES | JD | 1983 |
| JEFFREY R. PANKRATZ | JD | 1991 |
| JEANNE M. PICHT | JD | 1994 |
| BRUCE A. POLIZOTTO | JD | 1967 |
| TONY PRATHER | JD | 1983 |
| RAPHAEL M. PREVOT JR. | JD | 1984 |
| JOHN W. PURCELL | JD | 1976 |
| JANE E. RALEY | JD | 1982 |
| STEPHEN E. REYNOLDS | JD | 2008 |
| JOHN F. "JEFF" RICHARDSON | JD | 1977 |
| TIMOTHY J. RIFFLE | JD | 1983 |
| LAURIE ROBINSON HADEN | JD | 1998 |
| RYNTHIA MANNING ROST | JD | 1980 |
| ZALDWAYNAKA "Z" SCOTT | JD | 1983 |
| JOHN E. SEDDELMEYER | JD | 1974 |
| TAYLOR C. SEGUE III | JD | 1983 |

| | | |
|---|---|---|
| ELIZABETH SHUMAN-MOORE | JD | 1982 |
| SARAH M. SINGLETON | JD | 1974 |
| DAN E. SPICER | JD | 1973 |
| KELLYE Y. TESTY | JD | 1991 |
| MILTON O. THOMPSON | JD | 1979 |
| COURTNEY R. TOBIN | JD | 1992 |
| W. WILLIAM WEEKS | JD | 1979 |
| GENE WILKINS | JD | 1957 |
| BRIAN P. WILLIAMS | JD | 1981 |
| KENNETH R. YAHNE | JD | 1968 |
| C. DANIEL YATES | JD | 1973 |

# Sources

## Sources Cited

### Chapter 1

*Alumnus.* 1898–99. Bloomington: Indiana University Alumni Association.

Barbour, Humphrey M. 1920. "Indiana University in the Civil War." *Indiana University Alumni Quarterly* 7, no. 4 (October): 486–517.

*Catalogue.* 1845, 1847, 1877. Bloomington: Indiana University.

*Indiana Daily Student.* 1914–. Bloomington: Indiana University.

*Indiana Student.* 1867–94. Bloomington: Indiana Student.

Indiana University Board of Trustees Minutes. 1841, 1842. Accessed March 20, 2017. http://webapp1.dlib.indiana.edu/iubot/welcome.do.

*Laws of the State of Indiana.* 1819. Corydon, IN: A. and J. Brandon.

*Laws of the State of Indiana.* 1827. Corydon, IN: A. and J. Brandon.

*Laws of the State of Indiana.* 1837. Corydon, IN: A. and J. Brandon.

McDonald, David. 1843. *Introductory Address on the Study of Law Delivered on the Chapel of Indiana University.* Bloomington, IN: Marcus L. Deal.

Miller, Robert G. 1950. *Indiana University School of Law: Notes and Material Gathered for the Preparation of a History of the Law School of Indiana University.* https://www.repository.law.indiana.edu/cgi/viewcontent.cgi?article=1005&context=histdocs.

Woodburn, Robert. 1940. *History of Indiana University, Volume 1, 1820–1902.* Bloomington: Indiana University.

Wylie, Theophilus A. 1890. *Indiana University, Its History from 1820, When Founded, to 1890.* Indianapolis: Wm. B. Burford, Lithographer, Printer, and Binder.

### Chapter 2

*Arbutus.* 1896. Bloomington: Indiana University.

*Indiana Alumnus.* 1921–26. Bloomington: Indiana University Alumni Office.

*Indiana Daily Student.* 1914–. Bloomington: Indiana University.

*Indiana Student.* 1867–94. Bloomington: Indiana Student.

Myers, Burton Dorr. 1952. *History of Indiana University, Volume 2, 1902–1937.* Bloomington: Indiana University.

Pauwels, Colleen K. 2000. "Hepburn's Dream: The History of the Indiana Law Journal." *Indiana Law Journal* 75, no. 1 (Winter): i–xxxiii.

Reinhard, George L. 1904. "American Law Schools and the Teaching of Law." *Green Bag* 16, no. 3 (March): 165–70.

## Chapter 3

Gavit, Bernard C. 1950. "Where Do We Go from Here in Legal Education?" *Rocky Mountain Law Review* 23:24–33.

———. 1951. *Introduction to the Study of Law*. Brooklyn, NY: Foundation Press.

"Gavit Gives New Scholastic Rules for Law School." 1933. *Indiana Daily Student*, October 12, 4.

"I.U. Law School Ranks 14th in Enrollment." 1964. *Indianapolis Star*, May 27, 29.

## Chapter 4

*Indiana Lawyer*. 1990–. Indianapolis, IN: City Business/USA.

Indiana University News Room, News Archive. 2007–9, 2011. Accessed June 14, 2018. http://newsinfo.iu.edu/web/page/normal/1286.html?s=pages&n=5101.

Pauwels, Colleen K. 1992. "Inferior to None." *Bill of Particulars* (Fall): 15–36.

## Chapter 5

*Catalogue*. 1847. Bloomington: Indiana University.

*Daily Student*. 1898–1912. Bloomington, IN: Daily Student.

*Indiana Daily Student*. 1914–. Bloomington: Indiana University.

LeBus, Betty V. 1957. "A Law Building for Indiana University." *Law Library Journal* 50:213–16.

Lockridge, Ross. 1948. *Raintree County*. Boston: Houghton Mifflin.

Lowell, Mildred Hawksworth. 1957. "Indiana University Libraries, 1829–1942." PhD diss., University of Chicago.

Maurer School of Law. 2015. "Baier Hall and Jerome Hall Law Library Naming Ceremony." May 8, 2015. https://www.repository.law.indiana.edu/mle/3/.

## Chapter 6

*Bill of Particulars*. 1968–2006. Bloomington: Indiana University School of Law–Bloomington Alumni Association.

Clark, Thomas D. 1973. *Indiana University, Midwestern Pioneer, Volume 2: In Mid-Passage*. Bloomington: Indiana University Press.

*Daily Student*. 1898–1912. Bloomington, IN: Daily Student.

*Indiana Alumni Magazine*. 1938–. Bloomington: Indiana University Alumni Association.

Robinson, Greg. 2016. *The Great Unknown: Japanese American Sketches*. Boulder: University Press of Colorado.

Romero, Flerida. 2012. "Reaching for the Stars." In *In the Grand Manner: Looking Back, Thinking Forward*, edited by Danilo O. Concepcion, Marvic M. V. F. Leonen, Concepcion L. Jardeleza, and Florin T. Hilbay, 168–94. Diliman, Quezon City: University of the Philippines College of Law. https://www.scribd.com/doc/113199784/In-the-Grand-Manner-Looking-Back-Thinking-Forward.

# Other Sources Consulted

## Books and Articles

Boshkoff, Douglass G. 1976. "Indiana's Rule 13: The Killy-Loo Bird of the Legal World." *Learning and the Law* 3 (Summer): 19–20.

Boshkoff, Douglass G., et al. 1975. "Course Selection, Student Characteristics and Bar Examination Performance: The Indiana University Law School Experience." *Journal of Legal Education* 27:127–37.

Capshew, James H. 2012. *Herman B Wells: The Promise of the American University.* Bloomington: Indiana University Press.

Cate, Fred H., Dennis H. Long, and David C. Williams, eds. 2001. *The Court-Martial of George Armstrong Custer.* Bloomington: Indiana University School of Law.

Cate, Fred H., and David C. Williams, eds. 1997. *The Trial of Richard III.* Bloomington: Indiana University School of Law.

Clark, Thomas D. 1970. *Indiana University, Midwestern Pioneer, Volume 1: The Early Years.* Bloomington: Indiana University Press.

———. 1973. *Indiana University, Midwestern Pioneer, Volume 2: In Mid-Passage.* Bloomington: Indiana University Press.

———. 1977. *Indiana University, Midwestern Pioneer, Volume 3: Years of Fulfillment.* Bloomington: Indiana University Press.

Emerson, Thomas I. 1965. "Fowler Vincent Harper." *Yale Law Journal* 74:601–3.

Fariss, Linda K., ed. 1992. *150 Years of Research: A Bibliography of the Indiana University School of Law Faculty, 1842–1992.* Bloomington: Indiana University School of Law.

Gavit, Elizabeth N. 1980. *The Accomplishments of Bernard Campbell Gavit as Dean of Indiana University Law School.* Indianapolis, IN: Butler University.

"Lauren Robel." Forthcoming. In *The Trustees and Officers of IU, 1982–2018.* Bloomington: Indiana University.

"A New Era in Law Study." 1956. *Indiana Alumni Magazine* (January): 3–4.

Orosa, Mario E. 2018. "The Philippine Pensionado Story." Accessed May 5, 2018. http://www.orosa.org/The%20Philippine%20Pensinonado%20Story3.pdf.

Pauwels, Colleen K. 1992. "Inferior to None." *Bill of Particulars* (Fall): 15–36.

Sanders, Chauncey. 1939. "A Century of Education in Law at Indiana University." *Indiana Alumni Magazine* (October): 5–8, 31.

Sullivan, William M., et al. 2007. *Educating Lawyers: Preparation for the Profession of Law.* San Francisco: Jossey-Bass.

Wells, Herman B. 1980. *Being Lucky: Reminiscences and Reflections.* Bloomington: Indiana University Press.

## Indiana University Publications

*Alumnus.* 1898–99. Bloomington: Indiana University Alumni Association.

*Arbutus.* 1894–. Bloomington: Indiana University.
    Includes valuable information about activities of the law school, especially fraternities, clubs, and athletic events.

*Catalogue.* 1830–1950. Bloomington: Indiana University.
   Contains information about admission and graduation requirements as well as
   courses.
*Daily Student.* 1898–1912. Bloomington, IN: Daily Student.
*Indiana Alumni Magazine.* 1938–. Bloomington: Indiana University Alumni Association.
*Indiana Student.* 1867–94. Bloomington: Indiana Student.
*Indiana Student.* 1912–14. Bloomington: Indiana University.
*Indiana Daily Student.* 1914–. Bloomington: Indiana University.
   The student newspapers contain valuable information about the law school, especially
   during the early years of its existence. The Jerome Hall Law Library has digitized ar-
   ticles from the newspapers relating to the school from 1868 through 1931.
*Indiana University Alumni Quarterly.* 1914–38. Bloomington: Alumni Association of In-
   diana University.
*Student.* 1894–98. Bloomington: Publishing Association of Indiana University.


## School of Law Alumni Publications

The law school began publishing an alumni magazine in 1959. The titles have changed,
but each is a rich resource for the events of importance to the school's history.


*Alumni News.* 2007–9. Bloomington: Indiana University School of Law.
*Alumni Update.* 1998–2001. Bloomington: Indiana University School of Law.
*Annual Report of the Dean.* 1979–2017. Bloomington: Indiana University School of Law.
*Bill of Particulars.* 1968–2006. Bloomington: Indiana University School of Law–Bloom-
   ington Alumni Association.
*Ergo.* 2010–. Bloomington: Indiana University Maurer School of Law.
*The Exordium.* 1978–91. Bloomington: Indiana University School of Law.
*The I Witness.* 1959–68. Bloomington: Indiana University Law School Alumni Associa-
   tion.
*Indiana Law.* 2007–9. Bloomington: Indiana University School of Law.
*Indiana Law Update.* 2002–9. Bloomington: Indiana University School of Law.
*IU Law Update.* 1991–97. Bloomington: Indiana University School of Law.


## Print and Digital Archives

Indiana University Archives. Wells Library. http://webapp1.dlib.indiana.edu.
   The IU Archives contain folders about the law school, especially prior to 1950.
Indiana University Board of Trustees Minutes. http://webapp1.dlib.indiana.edu/iubot
   /welcome.do.
Indiana University News Room, News Archive. http://newsinfo.iu.edu/web/page/normal
   /1286.html?s=pages&n=5101.
Indiana University Photo Archive. http://webapp1.dlib.indiana.edu/archivesphotos/index
   .jsp.
Jerome Hall Law Library Archives, Baier Hall.
   The Jerome Hall Law Library contains the files for many of the deans as well as fac-
   ulty minutes, catalogs, brochures, and publications of the law school.

Jerome Hall Law Library Digital Repository. www.repository.law.indiana.edu.
    The digital repository contains a collection for the law school's history. Among the
    items in this collection are all the alumni publications, digitized sections of the *Ar-
    butus* concerning the law school, a biographical list of deans, a collection of notable
    graduates, commencement programs, dedication materials, and the Academy of Law
    Alumni Fellows brochures. The repository also includes a complete list of all publica-
    tions of the law faculty.

# *Index*

*Italicized page numbers refer to illustrations and sidebars.*

law, 87, 96, 131, 135, 137; requirements for, 28–29, 47, 58, 131

Delbrück, Jost, 85, *134*, 160

Delgado, Francisco A., 128, *129*

Delta Alpha Delta, 32

Delta Theta Phi, 32

Demurrer Club, 29–30

Dettmers, Hans Jurgen, *133*

Development and Alumni Affairs Building, 90

Dickerson, Reed, 62, 67–68

digitization of the library, 118, 122, 123–24

diplomas, 50–51

Distinguished Service Award, 143, 146, *180*, 181–83App4

diversity: faculty, 85, 87; student body, xv, 27, 67

doctoral programs: juridical science, doctor of (SJD), 137; Juris Doctor degree (JD), 32, 34, 58, 66, 90, 101, 131–32; law and democracy PhD, 137, 139

Dunham, Allison, 57

Dunn's Woods, 17–18, 19, 79

Dutton, Ben, 57

Dworkin, Roger, 65–66

Eaglin, Jessica, 98

Eggleston, Miles G., 5

Ehrlich, Thomas, 83

Elmore, David, 90–91, *145*

Elmore, D. G., Jr., 90–91

Elmore Entrepreneurship Law Clinic, 90–91

endowed chairs, 64, *100*

enrollment: in the 1960s, 63, 67; Civil War, 12; early 20th century, 23–24, 27, 29; in the early years, 6–7, 14; female, 54, 59; post-WWII jump in, 57; twenty-first century, 102; during World War I, 34; during World War II, 54

entertainers, alumni as, 163

Entrepreneurship Law Clinic, 90–91

Eschbach, Jesse, 64, *147*

European students, 133–35

Evening Division, Indianapolis, 66–67

Evens, Alfred, 47

externships, 86, 96, 101

faculty: 1915, *30*; in 1969, 67; 1978–79, 75; 2006–2007, 91; 2016–2017, *101*; diversity of, 85, 87; in the early years, 9, 11–13; in globalization, xvi, 75, 77; in growing reputation, 48–50; on the *Indiana Law Journal*, 39; in the mid-1980s, 82; in national standards, 35, 38; post-WWII expansion of, 57; in the rebirth of the law school, 41–42; in reinstatement of the law school, 18; scholarship by, 41, 47, 49–50, *51*, *56*, 67–68, 75; visiting, in globalization, 85; in World War II, 54. *See also under name of faculty member*

Family and Mediation Clinic, 92

Fariss, Linda K., *122*, 123–24

Farnsworth, Lisa, 139

*Federal Communications Law Journal*, 87

fellowships, 85

Fidler, David, 85, *100*

financial difficulties: in the 1800s, xv–xvi, 9; in the 1970s, xv–xvi; Depression-era, 45–46; in failure to grow, 42; for the library, 108, 109, 111, 114, 116–17; and reputation building, 62–63; in suspension of the law department, 14–15

First College Building, *3*, *5*, 13, 105

Fischman, Rob, 85, *100*

Fitzgerald, Nathan Ward, *144*

Fitzpatrick, James, 87, 90

Fletcher, Gina-Gail, 98

Foohey, Pamela, 98

football, *36*, *37*

foreign students, xv, 127–37, *127*, *131*

foreign study, 86, 96

Forum Court, 19, *20*, *21*

Fox, Merritt, 77

Frank, John Paul, 57

fraternities, 32

Friedlander, Ezra H., *148*

Fromm, Leonard D., 76, 77

Fuchs, Ralph, *56*, 57

Fuentes-Rohwer, Luis, 87

Gamage, David, 98

Gamma Eta Gamma, 32

Garrard, William I., *148*

38; need to expand, 74; in the new Law Building, 116; owl and squirrel in, *125*; party for graduating students in, *120*; personal papers deposited in, 124; reading room, *111, 114*; renamed Jerome Hall Law Library, 97, *123*, 124; space issues in, 116–18, 119–20; students staffing, 108–9; as Supreme Court records depository, 116; voted "best law library," *121*; in Wylie Hall, 106–7, *107*. *See also* Jerome Hall Law Library

Library Hall, 19

Lilly Endowment/Foundation, xvi, 77–78, 91–92

Lockridge, Ross Franklin, 109

Lofti, Azin, 90

London Law Consortium, 86

Long, Dennis, 90

Long, Robert, 90

Lopez, Arthur, *151*

Lovelace, Timothy, 95

Madeira, Jody, 91–92, 99

Mad Monks of Maxwell, 36, 59

Mann, Howard, 5, 57

Mann, J. Keith, 159

masters degrees: master of comparative law (MCL), 135; master of laws degree (LLM), 87, 96, 131, 137

Mattioli, Michael, 95

Maurer, Janie, 92, *92*, 94

Maurer, Mickey, xvi, 89, 92, *92*, *93*, 94, *144*

Maxwell Hall: in 1898, *17*; classroom in, 1942, *52*; exterior of, *27, 35*; library in, 107–8, *111, 112*; move to, 1908, 28; Phi Delta Phi class of 1942, *53*

McAtee, Jesse W., *110*

McCarthyism, 55, *56*, 57

McDonald, David, xv, 3, 6–7, *7*, 9, 11, 105

*McDonald's Treatise* (McDonald), 7

McGuffey, William Holmes: "Mcguffey's Reader," 30, 32

McNutt, Paul V., 39–41, *40*, 45–46, 57, 157

McRobbie, Michael, 91, 92, *92*, 94, 97

media, alumni in, *144*

medical school rivalry, 36

Medine, David, 83

Mehrotra, Ajay, 91–92

Mellette, Arthur C., 15, 152

Merced, Felino Lorenzo, 131

Meyer, Alfred, 62

Meyer, James, 34

Miers, Robert W., 14

military service, 53

Milt and Judi Stewart Center on the Global Legal Profession, 86

Milton Stewart Fellows Overseas Externship Program, 86

Minton, Sherman, *31*, 42, *57*, 62, 109, 146–47, 155

miscegenation laws, 128, 131

Miyakawa, Masuji, 27, *130*, 131

mock trials: court-martial of George Armstrong Custer, 88, 90; in Forum Court, 21; trial of Richard III, *87*, 88, 90

moot courtrooms, *23, 31*, 61–62, *87*, *88*, 90

Morehead, Andrea, *144*

Moss, Lemuel, 14–15

Murray, William Pitt, 8, 9, 11

Nagy, Donna, 91–92, *100*

*National Jurist* magazine, *121*

Need, Mark, 91–92

Neff, Francis, 11

New Deal programs, 48

Newsom, Floyd, *107*

newspaper editors, alumni as, *144*

Nolan, Val, 57, 71, 74, 78, 157–58

Nuremberg Trials, *151*

Nutt, Cyrus, *12*

O'Bannon, Frank, 152–53, 155

O'Byrne, Estella, 83

O'Byrne, Roscoe, 34, 83

Ochoa, Christiana, 91–92, *100*

Old Crescent, 1898, *17*

Oliver, Bill, 62

Onada, John, *144*

O'Neil, Robert M., 71

Order of the Coif, 38

Orenstein, Aviva, 85

Otto, William T., 7, 9, 11

Owen Hall, *17*, 19

LINDA K. FARISS is Director Emerita of the Jerome Hall Law Library and a 1988 graduate of the Maurer School of Law. Prior to her retirement in early 2017, Fariss served in various capacities at the Jerome Hall Law Library over a forty-year career, including Law Library Director and Senior Lecturer in Law from 2011 until February 2017. In addition to articles on law librarianship, Fariss, along with her colleagues Keith Buckley and Colleen K. Pauwels, authored *Legal Research: Traditional Sources, New Technology.*

KEITH BUCKLEY is Director of the Jerome Hall Law Library and a 1989 graduate of the Maurer School of Law. In his forty years with the Jerome Hall Law Library, Buckley has served in a number of capacities, from Reference Librarian to Law Library Director beginning in 2017. Buckley authored *Legal Research: Traditional Sources, New Technology* with his colleagues Linda K. Fariss and Colleen K. Pauwels, and *Indiana Stonecarver: The Story of Thomas R. Reding* with Ann Nolan.